The
PLC+
Playbook

The

PLC+
Playbook

A HANDS-ON GUIDE TO COLLECTIVELY
IMPROVING STUDENT LEARNING
GRADES K–12

A COMPANION TO
PLC+
BETTER DECISIONS
AND GREATER IMPACT
BY DESIGN

NAME _____

SCHOOL/ORGANIZATION _____

Douglas Fisher • Nancy Frey • John Almarode
Karen Flories • Dave Nagel

FOR INFORMATION:

Corwin

A SAGE Company

2455 Teller Road

Thousand Oaks, California 91320

(800) 233-9936

www.corwin.com

SAGE Publications Ltd.

1 Oliver's Yard

55 City Road

London EC1Y 1SP

United Kingdom

SAGE Publications India Pvt. Ltd.

B 1/I 1 Mohan Cooperative Industrial Area

Mathura Road, New Delhi 110 044

India

SAGE Publications Asia-Pacific Pte. Ltd.

18 Cross Street #10-10/11/12

China Square Central

Singapore 048423

Director and Publisher, Corwin Classroom: Lisa Luedeke

Editorial Development Manager: Julie Nemer

Senior Editorial Assistant: Sharon Wu

Production Editor: Melanie Birdsall

Copy Editor: Cate Huisman

Typesetter: C&M Digitals (P) Ltd.

Proofreader: Sarah J. Duffy

Cover and Interior Designer: Gail Buschman

Marketing Manager: Deena Meyer

Printed in the United States of America

Library of Congress Cataloging-in-Publication Data

Names: Fisher, Douglas, author.

Title: The PLC+ playbook, grades K-12 : a hands-on guide to collectively improving student learning / Douglas Fisher, Nancy Frey, John Almarode, Karen Flories, Dave Nagel.

Other titles: PLC plus playbook

Description: Thousand Oaks, California : Corwin, 2019. | Includes bibliographical references.

Identifiers: LCCN 2019008218 | ISBN 9781544378442 (pbk. : alk. paper)

Subjects: LCSH: Professional learning communities. | Teaching teams. | Academic achievement.

Classification: LCC LB1731 .F487 2019 | DDC 370.71/1—dc23

LC record available at https://lccn.loc.gov/2019008218

This book is printed on acid-free paper.

21 22 23 10 9 8

CONTENTS

List of Videos   xiii

About the Authors   xiv

Acknowledgments   xvi

Welcome to the PLC+ Playbook   xvii

MODULE 1: THE PURPOSE AND STATUS OF YOUR PLC+   1

Put the Playbook to Work for You   1

PLC Defined   1

PLC+ Guiding Questions   8

MODULE 2: CROSSCUTTING VALUES AND OPPORTUNITIES TO GROW YOUR PLC+ TEAM   11

Put the Playbook to Work for You   11

Crosscutting Values   11

SWOT Analysis   15

MODULE 3: ON YOUR OWN: THE PLUS IS YOU   19

Put the Playbook to Work for You   19

Your Individual Identity   20

Teacher Credibility   21

Teacher Credibility and Its Intersection
    With Crosscutting Values   23

Teacher Self-Efficacy   25

Teacher Self-Efficacy and Its Intersection
    With Crosscutting Values   26

MODULE 4: COLLECTIVE EFFICACY AND CREDIBILITY IN A PLC+ 29

Put the Playbook to Work for You 29

Revisiting Teacher Credibility and Teacher Self-Efficacy 29

From Individual to Collective Teacher Efficacy 33

Setting Norms for Our Ways of Work 35

Norms for Our Ways of Work in Our PLC+ 37

MODULE 5: GUIDING QUESTION I: WHERE ARE WE GOING? ANALYZE STANDARDS 39

Put the Playbook to Work for You 39

Analyzing Standards 40

Design the Learning Progression 42

Develop Daily Learning Intentions 45

Identify Success Criteria 48

Complete PLC+ Template for Guiding Question 1: Where Are We Going? 50

MODULE 6: WHERE ARE WE GOING? CROSSCUTTING VALUES CHECK 51

Put the Playbook to Work for You 51

Equity and Expectations Values Checklist 51

Activate Learning for Myself and Others Checklist 53

Collective Efficacy Checklist 54

MODULE 7: GUIDING QUESTION 2: WHERE ARE WE NOW? DATA COLLECTION 55

Put the Playbook to Work for You 55

Initial Assessment Data Collection 56

Data Gathering 61

MODULE 8: WHERE ARE WE NOW? DATA ANALYSIS, COMMON CHALLENGES, AND MISCONCEPTION ANALYSIS   63

Put the Playbook to Work for You   63

Data Analysis Protocol   64

Common Challenge Protocol   67

Identify Student Misconceptions   71

MODULE 9: WHERE ARE WE NOW? CROSSCUTTING VALUES CHECK   73

Put the Playbook to Work for You   73

Equity and Expectations Values Checklist   73

Activate Learning for Myself and Others Checklist   75

Collective Efficacy Checklist   76

MODULE 10: GUIDING QUESTION 3: HOW DO WE MOVE LEARNING FORWARD? STRENGTHENING OUR TEACHING PRACTICES   77

Put the Playbook to Work for You   77

Pair Teaching Strategies With Evidence Gathering   78

Coaching Corners Protocol   81

MODULE 11: HOW DO WE MOVE LEARNING FORWARD? ASSIGNMENT ANALYSIS   83

Put the Playbook to Work for You   83

Assignment Analysis Tool   84

MODULE 12: HOW DO WE MOVE LEARNING FORWARD? LEARNING WALKS — 87

Put the Playbook to Work for You — 87

What Is a Learning Walk? — 87

Types of Learning Walks and Their Purposes — 88

MODULE 13: HOW DO WE MOVE LEARNING FORWARD? MICROTEACHING — 95

Put the Playbook to Work for You — 95

Microteaching in a Professional Learning Community — 95

Preparation for Microteaching: The Volunteer Teacher — 97

MODULE 14: HOW DO WE MOVE LEARNING FORWARD? CROSSCUTTING VALUES CHECK — 99

Put the Playbook to Work for You — 99

Equity and Expectations Values Checklist — 100

Activate Learning for Myself and Others Checklist — 101

Collective Efficacy Checklist — 102

MODULE 15: GUIDING QUESTION 4: WHAT DID WE LEARN TODAY? — 103

Put the Playbook to Work for You — 103

Build the Habit of Reflection — 104

MODULE 16: WHAT DID WE LEARN TODAY? BUILD EXPERT NOTICING — 109

Put the Playbook to Work for You — 109

Expert Noticing: How Is Our PLC+ Using Student Evidence of Learning? — 109

Expert Noticing Video Protocol — 110

Noticing Note-Taking Guide — 113

MODULE 17: WHAT DID WE LEARN TODAY? COMMON ASSESSMENTS

115

Put the Playbook to Work for You   115

Common Assessments/Quality Assessment Evidence   115

Design a Common Assessment to Use for Preunit and
Postunit Comparisons   118

MODULE 18: WHAT DID WE LEARN TODAY? DETERMINING IMPACT AND COMPARING PROGRESS AND ACHIEVEMENT

121

Put the Playbook to Work for You   121

Determining Impact   121

Progress Versus Achievement   121

Visualizing Data   122

MODULE 19: WHAT DID WE LEARN TODAY? CROSSCUTTING VALUES CHECK

125

Put the Playbook to Work for You   125

Equity and Expectations Values   125

Overcoming Obstacles to Talking About Learning   125

Equity and Expectations Values Checklist   128

Activate Learning for Myself and Others Checklist   129

Collective Efficacy Checklist   130

MODULE 20: GUIDING QUESTION 5: WHO BENEFITED AND WHO DID NOT BENEFIT?

131

Put the Playbook to Work for You   131

On Your Own   132

Data Review   135

On Your Own   136

Equity Audit Protocol: Revisit the Data as a Team   137

MODULE 21: WHO BENEFITED AND WHO DID NOT BENEFIT? RESPONDING TO IMPROVE STUDENT LEARNING 145

Put the Playbook to Work for You 145

The Vital Nature of Progress Monitoring 145

Tiered Intervention Progress Monitoring Protocol 146

MODULE 22: WHO BENEFITED AND WHO DID NOT BENEFIT? CROSSCUTTING VALUES CHECK 149

Put the Playbook to Work for You 149

Equity and Expectations Values Checklist 149

Activate Learning for Myself and Others Checklist 151

Collective Efficacy Checklist 152

References 155

Visit the companion website at
resources.corwin.com/plcplaybook
for downloadable resources and videos.

LIST OF VIDEOS

Note From the Publisher: The authors have provided video and web content throughout the book that is available to you through QR (quick response) codes. To read a QR code, you must have a smartphone or tablet with a camera. We recommend that you download a QR code reader app that is made specifically for your phone or tablet brand.

Videos may also be accessed at **resources.corwin.com/plcplaybook**

Video 1:   Overview of the PLC+ Playbook

Video 2:   Module 1 Introduction

Video 3:   Module 2 Introduction

Video 4:   Module 3 Introduction

Video 5:   Module 4 Introduction

Video 6:   Module 5 Introduction

Video 7:   Module 6 Introduction

Video 8:   Module 7 Introduction

Video 9:   Module 8 Introduction

Video 10:   Module 9 Introduction

Video 11:   Module 10 Introduction

Video 12:   Module 11 Introduction

Video 13:   Module 12 Introduction

Video 14:   Module 13 Introduction

Video 15:   Module 14 Introduction

Video 16:   Module 15 Introduction

Video 17:   Module 16 Introduction

Video 18:   Module 17 Introduction

Video 19:   Module 18 Introduction

Video 20:   Module 19 Introduction

Video 21:   Module 20 Introduction

Video 22:   Module 21 Introduction

Video 23:   Module 22 Introduction

ABOUT THE AUTHORS

Douglas Fisher, PhD, is Professor of Educational Leadership at San Diego State University and a leader at Health Sciences High and Middle College. He has served as a teacher, language development specialist, and administrator in public schools and nonprofit organizations, including 8 years as the Director of Professional Development for the City Heights Collaborative, a time of increased student achievement in some of San Diego's urban schools. Doug has engaged in Professional Learning Communities for several decades, building teams that design and implement systems to impact teaching and learning. He has published numerous books on teaching and learning, such as *Developing Assessment-Capable Visible Learners* and *Engagement by Design.* He can be reached at dfisher@sdsu.edu.

Nancy Frey, PhD, is a Professor of Educational Leadership at San Diego State University and a leader at Health Sciences High and Middle College. She has been a special education teacher, reading specialist, and administrator in public schools. Nancy has engaged in Professional Learning Communities as a member and in designing schoolwide systems to improve teaching and learning for all students. She has published numerous books, including *The Teacher Clarity Playbook* and *Rigorous Reading.* She can be reached at nfrey@sdsu.edu.

John Almarode, PhD, is an Associate Professor of Education at James Madison University, the Co-Director of the Center for STEM Education Outreach and Engagement, and the Director of the Content Teaching Academy. Prior to his work with schools, he served as a mathematics and science teacher in Virginia. John has engaged in professional learning with teachers and instructional leaders across the globe, integrating the science of how we learn into classrooms in all content areas and across all grade levels. He has published numerous books on teaching and learning, such as *Clarity for Learning* and *From Snorkelers to Scuba Divers*. He can be reached at almarojt@jmu.edu.

Karen Flories, MS Ed, is a full-time Professional Learning Consultant for Corwin and works with teachers and leaders across the nation. Prior to her role with Corwin, Karen was the Executive Director of Educational Services and Director of Literacy and Social Studies in Valley View School District, after serving as the English Department Chair for Romeoville High School. Karen's classroom experience includes high school English, special education, and alternative education. She has co-authored several books, including student learner notebooks on *Becoming an Assessment-Capable Visible Learner* for Grades 3–5 and 6–12. She can be reached at karen.flories@corwin.com.

Dave Nagel, MS Ed, is a full-time Professional Learning Consultant with Corwin. Dave has been a professional developer both nationally and internationally since 2003, working deeply with schools in the areas of assessment, improved grading and feedback actions to promote student learning, instructional leadership, and effective collaboration focused on ensuring both student and adult learning. Dave has done significant research related to effective collaboration and has developed practical instruments to assist collaborative teams in monitoring their adult behaviors to ensure having an effective team. In addition to his professional development work with teachers, leaders, community members, and other stakeholders, Dave is also a frequent speaker at state and national conferences and has contributed to several books, including *Effective Grading Practices for Secondary Teachers,* and published articles. He can be reached at dave.nagel@corwin.com.

ACKNOWLEDGMENTS

Corwin gratefully acknowledges the contributions of the following reviewers:

Dan Alpert
Program Director and Publisher, Equity and Professional Learning
Corwin
San Francisco, CA

Olivia Amador
Leader and Educational Consultant
San Diego, CA

Janice Bradley
Assistant Director, Utah Education Policy Center
University of Utah
Salt Lake City, UT

Amy Colton
Executive Director and Senior Consultant
Learning Forward Michigan
Ann Arbor, MI

Carol Flenard
Assistant Superintendent of Instruction
Spotsylvania County Public Schools
Fredericksburg, VA

Constance Hamilton
Author, Consultant, and Curriculum Director
Saranac Community Schools
Caledonia, MI

Dominique Smith
Chief of Educational Services and Teacher Support
Health Sciences High & Middle College
San Diego, CA

WELCOME TO THE PLC+ PLAYBOOK

DEAR EDUCATOR,

Many of us express gratitude to active and retired men and women who have served in the armed forces. We say, "Thank you for your service." We are grateful for the sacrifices they have made on behalf of all of us. And we believe that educators should also receive similar expressions of thanks from members of the public. As a teacher or administrator, you have dedicated your life to cultivating our most precious resource—other people's children. So let us be the first to say, "Thank you for your service." As a member of a caring profession, you have devoted your energy, creativity, and, at times, heartache to ensuring that children and adolescents thrive in your presence. No one got into this profession because he or she thought it would be an easy ride.

But it is also unfair to somehow expect that working *harder* is the answer to accelerating student learning and teacher professionalism. The solution is to work *wiser*. Although we can't take away all the toil, we designed PLC+ to equip professional learning communities with the tools they need to work more wisely.

This Playbook was designed to be an accompanying resource to the companion book *PLC+: Better Decisions and Greater Impact by Design*. It should serve as an aid in bringing the PLC+ framework to life. The modules in this Playbook are linked to the ideas and concepts discussed in the chapters of the book, and the activities have been designed to engage team members in deeper learning around those. Tools to support implementation of the PLC+ framework are embedded throughout the Playbook, and the four PLC+ crosscutting values are a common through line explored in each section. It is not expected that every team engaging in becoming a PLC+ will complete each activity in the Playbook. Rather, teams can find their appropriate entry point and use the applicable tools to help continue to develop their PLC+.

Once again, thank you for your service. You make an immeasurable difference in the lives of the students you teach, the colleagues you collaborate with, and the communities you serve.

With gratitude,

Doug, Nancy, John, Karen, and Dave

◄ **VIDEO 1: OVERVIEW OF THE PLC+ PLAYBOOK**
resources.corwin.com/plcplaybook

To read a QR code, you must have a smartphone or tablet with a camera. We recommend that you download a QR code reader app that is made specifically for your phone or tablet brand.

Module 1
THE PURPOSE AND STATUS OF YOUR PLC+

PUT THE PLAYBOOK TO WORK FOR YOU

The opening module of the Playbook serves to help your professional learning community build foundational knowledge about PLC+. Teams that are already acquainted with the PLC+ framework do not need to repeat Modules 1 and 2 at the start of every inquiry cycle. However, as new team members join, we advise that you revisit this work in order to sustain core knowledge. This module presents information about the characteristics of high-performing teams, followed by discussion of the five PLC+ guiding questions that drive your work. The purpose of this module is for teams to unearth assumptions about how professional learning communities work, and to promote the use of a shared vocabulary for professional inquiry and action.

PLC DEFINED

Take a moment to read the following quote by Shirley Hord (2007). As you read it, underline commonalities in what Hord describes as the purpose of a PLC, and the purposes that your team has captured. Circle anything that Hord mentions that resonates with you, whether it is confirmation of your current work, or aspirational:

A PLC is demonstrated by the collective learning that occurs. Professional staff from all departments and grade levels come together to study collegially and work collaboratively. They engage in collegial inquiry that includes reflection and discussion focused on instruction and student learning. They are continuously learning together. For example, a group may begin investigating student performance data to assess student successes and needs. Through reflection and discussion, the group identifies areas that need

◄ **VIDEO 2: MODULE 1 INTRODUCTION**
resources.corwin.com/plcplaybook

attention—areas where they need to learn new content or instructional strategies. The group then explores how they will learn the new content or strategies. The group members may decide they will learn from someone on staff, from a central office specialist, from a colleague at another school, or from an external consultant. After they have put what they learned into practice, the staff goes through another cycle of reflection, discussion, and assessment. In other words, the learning is ongoing.

The PLC structure is one of continuous adult learning, strong collaboration, democratic participation, and consensus about the school environment and culture and how to attain the desired environment and culture. In such a collegial culture, educators talk with one another about their practice, share knowledge, observe one another, and root for one another's success (Barth, 2006).

NOTES

_____

_____

_____

_____

_____

_____

_____

_____

_____

_____

_____

_____

_____

_____

_____

_____

_____

_____

TEAM TIME DISCUSSION

Discuss the concepts you and your team members circled. Which of these describe your current processes? Which are elements you are striving for?

Thus, the two main purposes, as noted in the introduction of the PLC+ book, are

1. To improve the pedagogical knowledge (skills and knowledge about how we teach) and the content knowledge (skills and knowledge about what we teach) of educators through collaboration between colleagues

2. To improve the learning outcomes of students

There are six evidence-based characteristics of PLCs (Hord, 2004). Each of these needs to be considered if professional learning communities are to thrive. While the presence of these characteristics in and of themselves won't necessarily mean a PLC is effective, they are important considerations that teams should discuss as they embark on the journey of improving student learning and teacher expertise. Take a moment to individually self-assess your current reality against each of the six characteristics using the rating system below.

4: This is systematically embedded within our PLC.

3: This exists but couldn't yet be considered systematized.

2: This happens randomly and is not commonplace.

1: This is not yet established in our PLC.

NOTES

_____

_____

_____

_____

_____

_____

_____

_____

_____

_____

_____

_____

_____

SIX CHARACTERISTICS OF AN EFFECTIVE PLC	CURRENT RATING
1. **Structural Conditions:** Does our PLC have established times that we are able to meet? Are there schedules in place that support collaboration and diminish isolation? Is there availability of needed resources?	4 3 2 1

Ideas for Maintaining or Strengthening This Characteristic

2. **Supportive Relational Conditions:** Is there trust and respect in place within our PLC that provides the basis for giving and accepting feedback in order to work toward improvement?	4 3 2 1

Ideas for Maintaining or Strengthening This Characteristic

3. **Shared Values and Vision:** Do members of the team have the same goal? Do they have shared beliefs about student learning and the ability of team members to impact student learning?	4 3 2 1

Ideas for Maintaining or Strengthening This Characteristic

(Continued)

(Continued)

SIX CHARACTERISTICS OF AN EFFECTIVE PLC	CURRENT RATING
4. **Intentional Collective Learning:** Does our PLC engage in discourse and reflection around sharing practices, knowledge, and skills to impact the growth and achievement of our students? Do we find ways to learn from each other or learn together?	4 3 2 1

Ideas for Maintaining or Strengthening This Characteristic

5. **Peers Supporting Peers:** Does our PLC support lifting each other up? Do we celebrate individual and group successes? Do we observe one another while engaged in practice to help others strengthen their practice?	4 3 2 1

Ideas for Maintaining or Strengthening This Characteristic

6. **Shared and Supportive Leadership:** Are power, authority, and decision making shared and encouraged between teachers and building leaders? Is there a positive relationship among administrators and teachers in the school, where all staff members grow professionally as they work toward the same goal?	4 3 2 1

Ideas for Maintaining or Strengthening This Characteristic

TEAM TIME DISCUSSION

Share your ideas for maintaining or strengthening each of the six characteristics. Identify three to five actions your PLC+ is committed to taking to do so.

PLC is not a new term or concept. There are most likely strengths that exist within your current PLC structure that will enhance the ideas and concepts captured in the PLC+ framework. The framework is designed to capitalize on what your PLC is already doing well while offering new and innovative ways to think about teaching and learning, with a focus on the students as well as the teacher. Take a moment to read about the five PLC+ guiding questions on the following two pages. As you read, think about the similarities and differences the PLC+ captures in relation to your existing PLC structure. Capture your thoughts in the table on page 10.

PLC+ GUIDING QUESTIONS

1. Where are we going?

This first question is critical. Teams that can answer this question have high levels of teacher clarity. They are keenly aware of the academic standards their students are held accountable to, and they have analyzed these standards to ensure a thorough understanding of the skills, concepts, and rigor level that lie within each standard. That clarity is used to drive the engineering of learning tasks so that evidence of student learning can be gathered and used to make instructional inferences moving forward. This work is often guided by pacing guides and supported with a variety of curricular resources.

2. Where are we now?

In order to answer this question, teams need to have evidence to determine current student proficiency and readiness levels against what they captured in the "Where are we going?" question above. This allows teams to determine appropriate entry points for instruction starting with where students are and moving them to where they need to be. This may require an inventory of existing assessments to identify current resources your team has access to, as well as determining the assessments that will need to be collaboratively designed by the team members. From there, teams identify a common challenge that will drive inquiry into their students' current learning needs.

3. How do we move learning forward?

This question focuses on our teaching practices and the means by which we learn from one another. Learning walks and microteaching are two effective ways to frame the ways in which we analyze our own teaching using the wisdom of peers. These are not the only ways to consider how to best move learning forward. We cross-examine the tasks that we have designed for our students by analyzing assignments for rigor and alignment to standards.

4. What did we learn today?

This is a question often asked of students that has just as much power when asked of the adults. Focusing on this question helps teams to synthesize the information discussed and the data reviewed to examine student progress and achievement. Posing this question to teams helps to ground actions and commitments moving forward. By the same notion, we have to acknowledge the simplicity but significance of this question: *If we gathered and met as a PLC and didn't learn anything, couldn't we have just emailed each other what we talked about?*

5. Who benefited and who did not benefit?

This question continues the examination of student progress and achievement. At times, students who are already at high levels of achievement are not focused on as much as students who possess large deficits in their learning. However, growth is something that all students deserve regardless of their current proficiency level. A focus on this question exposes both, thus guiding team members where to go next for each learner. This is an equity question, and addressing it ensures that factors such as race, socioeconomic status, or disability status aren't used as excuses that impede a student's ability to learn. Teams examine the supports designed for students in light of what is working and take action to improve what is not.

NOTES

TEAM TIME DISCUSSION

Where are there some new opportunities that the PLC+ framework offers to your existing PLC practices?

SIMILARITIES TO OUR EXISTING PLC STRUCTURE		DIFFERENCES FROM OUR EXISTING PLC STRUCTURE
	1. Where are we going?	
	2. Where are we now?	
	3. How do we move learning forward?	
	4. What did we learn today?	
	5. Who benefited and who did not benefit?	

Module 2
CROSSCUTTING VALUES AND OPPORTUNITIES TO GROW YOUR PLC+ TEAM

PUT THE PLAYBOOK TO WORK FOR YOU

The purpose of Module 2 is to highlight the values that ground the PLC+ framework. These four values—*equity, high expectations, individual and collective efficacy,* and *activation*—underpin the work of your team. As these deep values are rarely discussed in day-to-day operations of a school, it is essential that high-performing teams take the time to commit (and recommit) to consequential work, and to one another.

CROSSCUTTING VALUES

In addition to the five guiding questions of the PLC+ framework, we offer four cross-cutting values that should permeate the work of teams: equity, high expectations, individual and collective efficacy, and activation. Read each of the crosscutting values described in the Introduction of the companion book *PLC+: Better Decisions and Greater Impact by Design* on pages 9–11. Annotate the text to highlight definitions and descriptions that resonate with you.

Equity

High Expectations

Individual and Collective Efficacy

Activation

◀ **VIDEO 3: MODULE 2 INTRODUCTION**
resources.corwin.com/plcplaybook

TEAM TIME DISCUSSION

Share the concepts and descriptions that you highlighted in your independent reading. In what ways do these crosscutting values reflect the mission of your classroom? Your school? Your district?

These values should impact students' learning and your teaching. How might they do so? As an example, Nancy noted that the writing expectations for a group of students were low. She brought this observation to the team, and they discussed reasonable expectations for students who struggle. The conversation eventually moved to focus on compensatory and adaptive strategies that might help students move forward in their writing. There are many other examples of how these values facilitate conversations about changes that can be enacted.

TEAM TIME DISCUSSION

The crosscutting values are intrinsic to the work of educators. Consider how these values shape student learning as well as the professional growth of teachers. Record your team discussion in the columns below.

	THIS WILL SUPPORT STUDENT LEARNING BY . . .	THIS WILL SUPPORT MY TEACHING BY . . .
Equity: A PLC+ needs to be a place where information is processed to identify and apply appropriate and impactful evidence-based instructional practices and culturally responsive teaching that values the background of every student and helps prepare each of them for success. In addition to valuing the background of every student, we must leverage their backgrounds to enhance learning.		
High Expectations: Ensuring we create and maintain high expectations for all students is a critical component of the PLC+ framework. All students are held accountable to reaching the same bar, yet the pathway by which they arrive at mastery will oftentimes look different. This, of course, is intertwined with equity, as are all of the crosscutting values.		

(Continued)

(Continued)

	THIS WILL SUPPORT STUDENT LEARNING BY . . .	THIS WILL SUPPORT MY TEACHING BY . . .
Individual and Collective Efficacy: There is an incredible amount of brain power we can capitalize on when we take our individual capacity and contribute it to a collective whole. This model asks us to use our collective efficacy to create the belief that we can make an impact on each and every one of our students, and align our beliefs with actions to make it so.		
Activation: High-functioning PLC+ teams don't just happen by chance. They require deliberate efforts and structures to ensure they are efficient and focused. This requires skilled facilitation as well as participation. The PLC+ needs someone who keeps the team discussions focused on goals, and on what the team needs to do to move forward.		

TEAM TIME DISCUSSION

Share your ideas for maintaining or strengthening each of the four values. Identify three to five actions your PLC+ is committed to taking to do so.

SWOT ANALYSIS

Now that you have

- Explored the purpose of a professional learning community,
- Analyzed the five guiding questions of a PLC+, and
- Discussed the four crosscutting values,

we invite you to engage in a strengths/weaknesses/opportunities/threats (SWOT) analysis. A SWOT analysis will help your team determine the current reality of your professional learning community, so you can best determine how to move forward.

The questions that a SWOT analysis helps you to answer are these:

- What are the internal strengths and weaknesses of our team?
- What are the external opportunities and threats in our school system and its environment?

- Can any weaknesses be converted to strengths?
- Can any threats turn into opportunities?
- How can our PLC+ take advantage of its strengths and opportunities?

As a team, take a moment to talk through each of the four quadrants described in the analysis grid that follows. Remember to focus the SWOT analysis on the purpose of a PLC+, including the guiding questions and crosscutting values.

PLC+ SWOT ANALYSIS GRID

	HELPFUL	HARMFUL
INTERNAL	What are our STRENGTHS?	What are our WEAKNESSES?
EXTERNAL	Where are our OPPORTUNITIES?	Where are our THREATS?

TEAM TIME DISCUSSION

AS A RESULT OF OUR SWOT ANALYSIS, A GOAL FOR OUR TEAM IS

ACTIONS WE WILL COMMIT TO AS A TEAM TO MEET OUR ESTABLISHED GOAL AND REALIZE THE PURPOSE OF A PROFESSIONAL LEARNING COMMUNITY

NOTES

Module 3

ON YOUR OWN

The Plus Is You

PUT THE PLAYBOOK TO WORK FOR YOU

This module of the PLC+ Playbook focuses on the significant role that you as the teacher have on student learning. PLC models in the past have concentrated heavily on student learning but have not focused equally on the need for teacher learning. Therefore, this module will highlight key components of teaching that strengthen the collective efficacy and credibility of your PLC+.

This module should be completed individually by you before your team meets again to share individual insights collectively. The purpose of this module is to frame a way for you to reflect on your strengths, professional identity, and goals. You will have the opportunity to share with your colleagues later. A high-performing team is more than the sum of its parts. Each member brings unique experiences and perspectives that can contribute positively to the work of the collective. That said, it is important that each team member has an awareness of self.

◀ **VIDEO 4: MODULE 3 INTRODUCTION**
resources.corwin.com/plcplaybook

YOUR INDIVIDUAL IDENTITY

The plus in the PLC+ framework is YOU! You are a vital component in the equation needed for your students' success. Take a moment and reflect on who you are as an educator and what your role means to you. In the spaces below, capture words, phrases, or pictures that recognize the "plus" about who you are as a teacher. There are questions to help prompt your thinking, but anything you come up with can go in your plus. It's about YOU!

Why did you become an educator?

What makes you a great teacher?

What is your hope for your students?

What goals do you have for yourself as an educator?

TEACHER CREDIBILITY

You reflected on who you are as a teacher. How would your students respond to the following question: *How would you describe your teacher?*

Teacher credibility, defined as the belief students have that they will learn from you, has a powerful impact on learning, with an effect size of 0.90 (Hattie, 2012). Teachers with a high degree of teacher credibility project competence, are dynamic in their delivery, convey trust, and are responsive to students. Read pages 15–17 of the companion book *PLC+: Better Decisions and Greater Impact by Design* on teacher credibility, and complete the activity that follows.

SAY IT IN 10 WORDS OR FEWER!

- Refer to pages 15–17 in Chapter 1 of *PLC+: Better Decisions and Greater Impact by Design* that talk about each characteristic of teacher credibility.
- Capture the essence of each characteristic in 10 words or fewer.

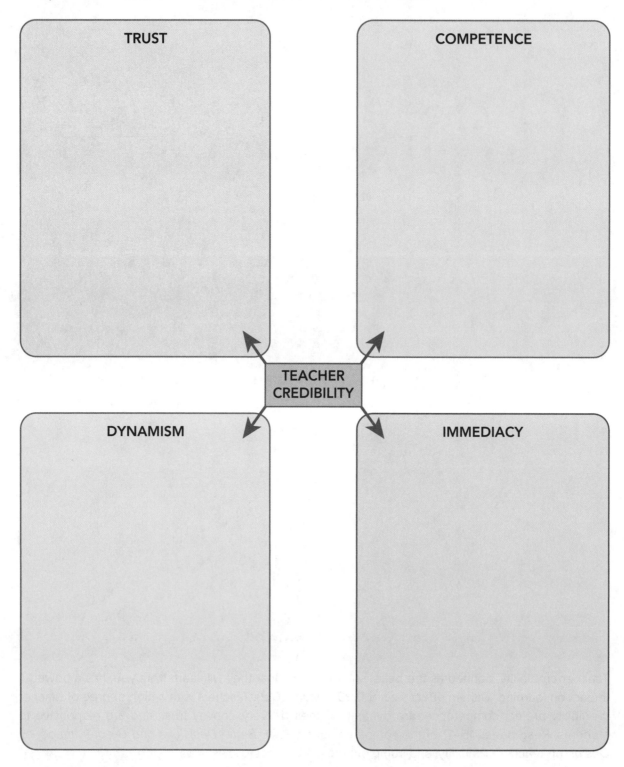

TRUST

COMPETENCE

TEACHER
CREDIBILITY

DYNAMISM

IMMEDIACY

TEACHER CREDIBILITY AND ITS INTERSECTION WITH CROSSCUTTING VALUES

The values woven into the fabric of a PLC+ are evidenced in the actions we take, the decisions we make, and language of learning we use with students and colleagues. Teacher credibility is influenced by the crosscutting values of equity, high expectations, individual and collective efficacy, and activation.

EVIDENCE WITH STUDENTS	I ENHANCE MY TEACHER CREDIBILITY WHEN I . . .	EVIDENCE WITH COLLEAGUES
	Address equity	
	Establish high expectations	
	Build efficacy	
	Activate learning for myself and others	

(Continued)

(Continued)

WAYS I CAN STRENGTHEN MY CREDIBILITY WITH STUDENTS THIS SCHOOL YEAR

WAYS I CAN STRENGTHEN MY CREDIBILITY WITH COLLEAGUES THIS SCHOOL YEAR

TEACHER SELF-EFFICACY

The collective efficacy of a team is derived from the individual efficacy of its members. In turn, the collective efficacy of the team positively influences one's individual sense of efficacy. This doesn't mean that each individual must believe that he or she is an expert about a particular topic. Rather, individual teacher efficacy is fostered by one's sense of self-capability. Highly self-efficacious teachers persist, are willing to employ multiple strategies to assist learners, and have warm positive interactions with students. Read pages 17–20 of *PLC+: Better Decisions and Greater Impact by Design* on teacher self-efficacy, and complete the activity below. Capture the essence of each factor by identifying one key word and one key phrase for each one.

EXPERIENCES OF MASTERY	MODELING
SOCIAL PERSUASION	PHYSIOLOGICAL FACTORS

What have you noticed about your own sense of self-efficacy? What experiences have you had that have contributed to your sense of self-efficacy? What experiences have lowered it?

EXPERIENCES THAT BUILD MY SELF-EFFICACY	EXPERIENCES THAT LOWER MY SELF-EFFICACY
•	•
•	•
•	•

TEACHER SELF-EFFICACY AND ITS INTERSECTION WITH CROSSCUTTING VALUES

The actions we take, the decisions we make, and language of learning we use with students and colleagues reflect the values woven into the fabric of a PLC+. Teacher self-efficacy is influenced by the crosscutting values of equity, high expectations, individual and collective efficacy, and activation.

EVIDENCE WITH STUDENTS	I BUILD MY TEACHER SELF-EFFICACY WHEN I . . .	EVIDENCE WITH COLLEAGUES
	Address equity	
	Establish high expectations	
	Build efficacy	
	Activate learning for myself and others	

WAYS I CAN STRENGTHEN MY SELF-EFFICACY IN MY INTERACTIONS WITH STUDENTS THIS SCHOOL YEAR

WAYS I CAN STRENGTHEN MY SELF-EFFICACY IN MY INTERACTIONS WITH COLLEAGUES THIS SCHOOL YEAR

NOTES

Module 4
COLLECTIVE EFFICACY AND CREDIBILITY IN A PLC+

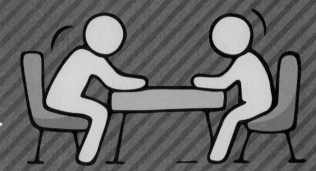

PUT THE PLAYBOOK TO WORK FOR YOU

In the previous module, you examined teacher credibility and teacher self-efficacy at the individual level. These factors influence the collective efficacy of your team. In addition, the quality of your team's work impacts your sense of self-efficacy.

In this module, your team will debrief your individual observations and consider these in light of collective teacher efficacy. You will develop a set of norms to govern your work going forward.

REVISITING TEACHER CREDIBILITY AND TEACHER SELF-EFFICACY

Effective professional learning communities communicate with one another. Debrief your insights about teacher credibility and teacher self-efficacy, and use the grid that follows to record brief notes on your colleagues' observations. A second grid is on the next page for use with larger teams.

◄ **VIDEO 5: MODULE 4 INTRODUCTION**
resources.corwin.com/plcplaybook

	TEAM MEMBER 1	TEAM MEMBER 2	TEAM MEMBER 3	TEAM MEMBER 4
What information was a surprise for you?				
What was confirmed for you?				
What was the most important thing you learned about yourself?				
What did you discover as being your greatest strength?				
What did you identify as being an area of growth for you?				
How can your teammates encourage and support you in the work of this PLC+?				

	TEAM MEMBER 5	TEAM MEMBER 6	TEAM MEMBER 7	TEAM MEMBER 8
What information was a surprise for you?				
What was confirmed for you?				
What was the most important thing you learned about yourself?				
What did you discover as being your greatest strength?				
What did you identify as being an area of growth for you?				
How can your teammates encourage and support you in the work of this PLC+?				

TEAM TIME DISCUSSION

Even colleagues that have worked together for many years learn new things about one another. How will your team use what you have learned in the future? What collective strengths will you attempt to build off of? What, if any, areas of growth were noted by the team?

FROM INDIVIDUAL TO COLLECTIVE TEACHER EFFICACY

Teams that are empowered to make decisions, act, communicate clearly, and hold themselves accountable for their efforts manifest high degrees of collective teacher efficacy (CTE). Collective teacher efficacy is defined by Goddard and Goddard (2001, p. 809) as "the perceptions of teachers in a school that the faculty as a whole can organize and execute the courses of action required to have a positive effect on students." Importantly, CTE is more than confidence. Read that quote again: "execute the courses of action required." That means seeking evidence of impact on student learning, and *responding when the impact is at less than desired levels.*

Professional learning communities raise their CTE through foundational commitments to the work (see Donohoo, 2017). Discuss the following PLC+ commitments. In what ways do each of these hold the potential to build CTE? What possible barriers should your team look for that might prevent CTE from growing?

NOTES

_____

_____

_____

_____

_____

_____

_____

_____

_____

_____

_____

_____

_____

_____

_____

_____

TEAM TIME DISCUSSION

WE RECOGNIZE THAT STUDENT LEARNING IS THE FOCUS.

Growth Opportunities	**Barriers to Avoid**

WE UNDERSTAND THAT SUSTAINED IMPROVEMENT REQUIRES A COLLECTIVE EFFORT.

Growth Opportunities	**Barriers to Avoid**

WE STICK TO WHAT THE DATA TELL US.

Growth Opportunities	**Barriers to Avoid**

WE ACCEPT THE DIFFICULT FACTS AND ACT ON THEM.

Growth Opportunities	**Barriers to Avoid**

WE NEED EACH OTHER TO TRULY ADDRESS THE NEEDS OF ALL OUR STUDENTS.

Growth Opportunities	**Barriers to Avoid**

SETTING NORMS FOR OUR WAYS OF WORK

High-performance teams develop and adhere to norms. Your classroom undoubtedly has norms that facilitate the ways you and your students work together. Review the work you have completed thus far in this Playbook, as it will assist you in developing a set of norms for your team. As a reminder, the analyses you have completed in this Playbook include the following:

- The characteristics of effective professional learning communities (pages 5–6)
- SWOT analysis (page 16)
- Your individual teacher credibility and teacher self-efficacy reflections (pages 21–27)
- Your team's insights about how knowledge of others will inform future work (pages 30–31)
- More information and examples can be found in the *The PLC+ Facilitation and Activator's Guide* by Dave Nagel.

Allow one hour for setting norms. While you might complete this activity in less time, it is important that you not rush. Larger groups may want to appoint a materials manager to organize, distribute, and collect items.

Materials:

- Index cards (8–10 for each team member)
- Black marker for each team member

Step 1: Distribute index cards and markers. Writing on only one side of the card, team members write down *one* group norm they would like to see. No more than one norm per card; participants can write as many cards as they like. No names are written on the cards. (5 minutes)

Step 2: Gather all the cards, shuffle them, and randomly redistribute them to team members. Each participant reads out loud the cards she or he has been given, and other team members share any cards that are the same or closely related to the one being read. As cards are read, they are collected by the materials manager and posted in groups that are similar (e.g., "respect," "disagreements," "agenda," etc.). Discussion is limited to grouping norms and identifying similarities between norms. (20 minutes)

Step 3: *Dissent option.* After the materials manager arranges all cards into categories (though some will be "stand-alones"), team members can propose to eliminate any norm. If one other participant "seconds" a proposal that a particular norm be eliminated, the index card of that norm is removed. (5 minutes)

Step 4: The team discusses condensing each group of norms into a single norm (without stringing them all together with the use of "and"). The goal is to create a single norm that captures the essence of the group of like ideas. (30 minutes)

Step 5: *Next steps.* The final product is a list of four to six group norms that will govern all discourse among the team. Record the agreed-upon norms on the following page. Hereafter, review the group norms at the beginning of every team meeting.

Source: Adapted from *The Practice of Authentic PLCs: A Guide to Effective Teacher Teams* by Daniel R. Venables (Corwin, 2011). Reprinted with permission from the publisher.

NOTES

_____

_____

_____

_____

_____

_____

_____

_____

_____

_____

_____

_____

_____

_____

_____

_____

_____

_____

_____

_____

_____

NORMS FOR OUR WAYS OF WORK IN OUR PLC+

MEMBERS

DATE

NORMS

-
-
-
-
-

NOTES

Module 5

GUIDING QUESTION 1: WHERE ARE WE GOING?

Analyze Standards

PUT THE PLAYBOOK TO WORK FOR YOU

The purpose of this module is to guide your team through a process of analyzing a standard (or standards) you will be teaching in an upcoming unit. Teams addressing the first guiding question in the PLC+ framework ("Where are we going?") closely examine the selected standards or curriculum objectives for the grade level or content area to identify key skills and concepts required for students to know and be able to do. The analyzed standard(s) then serves as a road map to develop learning progressions, learning intentions, and success criteria. The purpose is not to supplant the true work of a PLC+ team with lesson planning. Rather, the intention is for team members to understand what students need to learn and to ensure that there is a shared set of expectations for student learning. Modules 5 and 6 comprise tools for addressing "Where are we going?"

PLC+ Framework Guiding Questions

1. **Where are we going?**

2. **Where are we now?**

3. **How do we move learning forward?**

4. **What did we learn today?**

5. **Who benefited and who did not benefit?**

◄ **VIDEO 6: MODULE 5 INTRODUCTION**
resources.corwin.com/plcplaybook

ANALYZING STANDARDS

1. What are the concepts (nouns/noun phrases) in the standard? Underline the concepts in the standard.

2. What are the skills (verbs) in the standard? Circle the verbs in the standard.

ANALYSIS TEMPLATE EXAMPLE FOR THIRD GRADE

ELA-Literacy RI.3.2: (Determine) the main idea of a text; (recount) the key details and (explain) how they support the main idea.

CONCEPTS (NOUNS AND NOUN PHRASES)	SKILLS (VERBS)
Main idea of a text	Determine
Key details	Recount
How key details support main idea	Explain

YOUR SELECTED STANDARD

CONCEPTS IN YOUR SELECTED STANDARD (NOUNS AND NOUN PHRASES)	SKILLS IN YOUR SELECTED STANDARD (VERBS)

DESIGN THE LEARNING PROGRESSION

After you have analyzed the standard and there is agreement among the team about what students will need to learn, the learning progression is developed. The learning progression serves as the tentpoles for the unit, and includes major concepts and skills, as well as subskills of enabling knowledge whose absence might prevent a student from being able to meet the current standard(s). Gaps in student learning often occur because students failed to master skills and concepts in prior grades and/or content areas. Gaps also appear because teachers have not devoted time to ensure that the progression of learning is intentional and purposeful and builds upon prior learning. The logical question to ask is this: Does the learning progression scaffold and build learners' thinking as they progress toward proficiency and mastery of specific concepts and skills? Looking back at the standards that come before a grade level can support teams in identifying what some of the subskills are that may need to appear in the learning progression.

LEARNING PROGRESSIONS DISCUSSION EXAMPLE FOR THIRD GRADE ELA-LITERACY RI.3.2

QUESTION	NOTES
What prior knowledge is necessary for learners to successfully engage in this learning?	• Understand what a main idea is • Understand what a key detail is • Know how to include who/what/when/where/why/how evidence in their explanations (written and oral)
What skills and concepts did students need to master in prior standards?	**IN SECOND GRADE:** • Identify the main topic of a multiparagraph text • Identify the focus of specific paragraphs within the text
What learning experiences must they have to successfully build their prior learning and background knowledge?	• Oral explanations prior to written ones • Early practice with familiar texts

LEARNING PROGRESSIONS DISCUSSION EXAMPLE FOR THIRD GRADE ELA-LITERACY RI.3.2

QUESTION	NOTES
What scaffolding is necessary for all learners to successfully engage in this learning?	• Teacher modeling and think-alouds • Interactive reading aloud and shared reading instruction • Small group guided learning with more complex texts • Discuss with peers/reciprocal teaching
What do we know about students that can make these learning experiences more meaningful?	• Leverage science and social studies texts to reinforce this standard (teach with ELA focus in morning; content specific later in the day) • Winter holidays are approaching, so some of the informational texts can be about celebrations around the world

NOTES

_____

_____

_____

_____

_____

_____

_____

_____

_____

_____

_____

_____

_____

TEAM TIME DISCUSSION

YOUR SELECTED STANDARD

QUESTION	NOTES
What prior knowledge is necessary for learners to successfully engage in this learning?	
What skills and concepts did students need to master in prior standards?	
What learning experiences must students engage in to successfully build their prior learning and background knowledge?	
What scaffolding might be necessary for all learners to successfully engage in this learning?	
What do we know about our students that can make these learning experiences more meaningful?	

Survey of Resources: Are there additional instructional materials (curriculum maps, pacing guides, course instructor materials) or human resources (instructional coach, administrator, district curriculum director) that should be consulted to aid in our work?

RESOURCE	TEAM MEMBER RESPONSIBLE FOR OBTAINING RESOURCE

DEVELOP DAILY LEARNING INTENTIONS

Once the learning progression has been determined, the skills and concepts that were identified in the standards are used to develop learning intentions. Learning intentions provide transparency to the students about where they are going in their learning. There are three types of learning intentions captured below: content, language, and social. Content learning intentions answer the question "What am I learning today?" Language learning intentions delineate the literacy skills—reading, writing, speaking, and listening—that you will utilize in the lesson. Social learning intentions describe how students interact with their classroom community. Below is an example of one lesson's learning intentions the third-grade team developed. We also understand that some teams only focus on content learning intentions. *Other teams focus on all three aspects of learning.*

LEARNING INTENTIONS EXAMPLE FOR THIRD GRADE

CONTENT LEARNING INTENTION	Today we are learning how the key details of text help me understand the main idea of my reading.
LANGUAGE LEARNING INTENTION	Today we are reading the article "Magnets Everywhere," discussing our ideas, and writing a list of the key details.
SOCIAL LEARNING INTENTION	Today we are practicing careful listening to our classmates' ideas.

Notice that these three learning intentions draw from the lists of both concepts and skills generated in the analysis of the standard, as well as the supporting standards in the progression. One common misconception is that learning intentions come only from the nouns or concepts. Learning intentions are more than just restatements of the concepts or nouns of a standard. Instead, the content, language, and social learning intentions clearly state what students are learning, today, through the assimilation of concepts and skills during the learning experience or lesson. For example, drawing heavily from an analysis of this specific standard, students in the above classroom are learning about the relationship between the main idea and the key details of a text. The content learning intention brings the concepts of main idea and key details together with the skills *determine* and *list*. The language learning intention articulates the literacy demands and highlights the intended learning around the skills of determining and recounting using a specific text. Finally, the social learning intention will highlight the intended learning through explaining and listening to other classmates' ideas.

As you and your team move forward in developing your learning intentions, keep in mind that learning intentions

1. Articulate what learners are expected to learn through today's learning experience

2. Help learners see why they are learning this particular content and skills

These two features are both present in the above learning intentions. When asked, students in this classroom will know that they are learning about the main idea of a text and key details through active engagement with text and their peers. Why? So they can better understand what they are reading.

However, learning intentions should not

1. Be restatements of the standards

2. Focus solely on the concepts or nouns in the standard

NOTES

TEAM TIME DISCUSSION

Develop learning intentions for three lessons, derived from the standard you selected.

CONTENT LEARNING INTENTION	
LANGUAGE LEARNING INTENTION	
SOCIAL LEARNING INTENTION	

CONTENT LEARNING INTENTION	
LANGUAGE LEARNING INTENTION	
SOCIAL LEARNING INTENTION	

CONTENT LEARNING INTENTION	
LANGUAGE LEARNING INTENTION	
SOCIAL LEARNING INTENTION	

IDENTIFY SUCCESS CRITERIA

The usefulness of success criteria is threefold: (1) They bring into sharp focus the purpose for learning in the eyes of the teacher, thus improving teacher clarity; (2) they solidify shared understandings between teacher and students about what success looks like; and (3) they provide students, teachers, and PLC+ teams with a means to gauge progress of student learning. The success criteria need not change daily. However, they should be aligned to the concepts and skills identified in the standard. Success criteria are developed based on learning intentions that are derived from the standard.

SUCCESS CRITERIA EXAMPLE FOR THIRD GRADE

Standard: ELA-Literacy RI.3.2: Determine the <u>main idea of a text</u>; recount the <u>key details</u> and explain <u>how they support the main idea.</u>

SAMPLE LEARNING INTENTION	SAMPLE SUCCESS CRITERIA
• Today we are learning how the key details of text help me understand the main idea of my reading.	• I can describe or explain details such as who, what, when, where, and why from a text. • I can use key details to identify the main idea of a text.

Just as learning intentions do not solely focus on the concepts or nouns, success criteria are more than just the verbs in the standard. Instead, think of success criteria as the evidence learners are expected to produce that will allow them to gauge their progress and determine their level of mastery. For example, what will the learners in the above classroom be expected to do to make their learning visible around key details and the main idea of a text? They will be able to describe or explain details such as who, what, when, where, and why from a text and key details to identify the main idea of a text. These are the success criteria. Likewise, the teacher will be looking for this evidence during the learning experience so that adjustments can be made in real time.

As we will see in subsequent modules, clear success criteria, being transparent about the evidence of learning, will guide future conversations around moving learning forward, what we learned from today's lesson, and who did and did not benefit from our teaching. Clear success criteria, along with transparent learning intentions, lay the foundation for future work.

Standard

SAMPLE LEARNING INTENTION	SAMPLE SUCCESS CRITERIA
 • • • • • •	 • • • • • •

Standard

SAMPLE LEARNING INTENTION	SAMPLE SUCCESS CRITERIA
 • • • • • •	 • • • • • •

Standard

SAMPLE LEARNING INTENTION	SAMPLE SUCCESS CRITERIA
 • • • • • •	 • • • • • •

COMPLETE PLC+ TEMPLATE FOR GUIDING QUESTION 1: WHERE ARE WE GOING?

Standard

CONCEPTS (NOUNS AND NOUN PHRASES)	SKILLS (VERBS)
SAMPLE LEARNING INTENTION	SAMPLE SUCCESS CRITERIA

LEARNING PROGRESSION QUESTIONS	NOTES
What prior knowledge is necessary for learners to successfully engage in this learning?	
What skills and concepts did students need to master in prior standards?	
What learning experiences must students have to successfully build on their prior learning and background knowledge?	
What scaffolding is necessary for all learners to successfully engage in this learning?	
What do we know about our students that can make these learning experiences more meaningful?	

Module 6

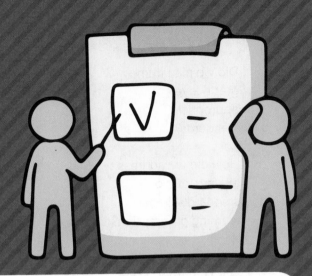

WHERE ARE WE GOING?
Crosscutting Values Check

PUT THE PLAYBOOK TO WORK FOR YOU

The purpose of this module is to check in on the extent to which crosscutting values of the PLC+ framework are realized in your work. This type of module will appear throughout the Playbook at the end of each guiding question. The crosscutting values check allows teams to make adjustments to improve learning for students and teachers.

EQUITY AND EXPECTATIONS VALUES CHECKLIST

The core values of the PLC+ framework include equity and expectations. Without these values, student learning varies considerably, and often students are blamed for their lack of progress or achievement. Members of a PLC+ team assume responsibility for the learning of all students and are willing to talk honestly, and openly, about how they can best meet the needs of all of their students. We are not suggesting that teachers have to know everything and meet every need. Together, we're better. And when we directly discuss the values of equity and expectations, we may uncover assumptions that need to be addressed. The following checklist provides some questions that PLC+ teams have found useful in checking in on their values.

◄ **VIDEO 7: MODULE 6 INTRODUCTION**
resources.corwin.com/plcplaybook

QUESTION	MY THOUGHTS	OUR COLLECTIVE THOUGHTS
Did we plan from grade-level-appropriate standards?		
How did we address all parts of the standard(s) in our learning progression?		
In what ways will the learning progression apply to all students?		
How have we considered accommodations and modifications for students who need them?		
Do we expect all students to reach mastery of the standards?		
In what ways are the tasks we use appropriately rigorous to ensure students have the experiences necessary to master the standards?		
What is our plan to address learning gaps that we identify?		
What is our plan to accelerate student learning as appropriate?		

ACTIVATE LEARNING FOR MYSELF AND OTHERS CHECKLIST

Student learning needs drive adult learning needs. Once we've established teacher clarity through analysis of standards and through design of learning progressions, learning intentions, and success criteria, teams need to take a step back to reflect on their personal learning. Are there any adult learning needs that must be met to best be able to support student learning? As already discussed, the + in the PLC+ is you, and so it is important to recognize learning for teachers is a constant. Doctors *practice* medicine, lawyers *practice* law. Why should it be any different for teachers? Teaching is a complex profession with many moving parts. Just as you wouldn't want your doctor ignoring advances in medicine and new ways to support health, the same holds true for teachers. We know more today than we did 30 years ago, and we will continue to know more as we move into the future. Absorbing that requires learning.

WHAT ARE THE LEARNING NEEDS OF MY STUDENTS?	WHAT ARE MY LEARNING NEEDS SO I CAN MEET MY STUDENTS' LEARNING NEEDS?	WHAT LEARNING WILL I ENGAGE IN TO MEET MY LEARNING NEEDS?
What do students need to learn?	What strategies might I need to learn more about?	What will I do on my own? What can I do with colleagues?

COLLECTIVE EFFICACY CHECKLIST

Teams that are empowered to make decisions, act, communicate clearly, and hold themselves accountable for their efforts manifest high degrees of collective teacher efficacy (CTE). Use the checklist below to gauge and monitor the actions that will follow your work about the first guiding question, "Where are we going?"

QUESTION	MY THOUGHTS	OUR COLLECTIVE THOUGHTS
Have we made plans to visit each other's classrooms to focus on teaching *and* learning? Are we willing to challenge each other to become stronger in our craft?		
How will we share the work we have done with others in the school?		
Do we have confidence in our ability to guide all students to meet standards?		
Are we prepared and committed to take action to move student learning forward? How will we accomplish this?		

Module 7

GUIDING QUESTION 2: WHERE ARE WE NOW?

Data Collection

PUT THE PLAYBOOK TO WORK FOR YOU

Once the team has identified where they are going, there needs to be an examination of current student performance. Modules 7–9 of the Playbook are designed to assist your team in answering the second PLC+ guiding question, "Where are we now?" Data collection and initial analysis are central in Module 7. Eliciting the right evidence drives the instructional inferences a team is able to make so they can continue to move learning forward.

PLC+ Framework Guiding Questions

1. Where are we going?
2. Where are we now?
3. How do we move learning forward?
4. What did we learn today?
5. Who benefited and who did not benefit?

◄ **VIDEO 8: MODULE 7 INTRODUCTION**
resources.corwin.com/plcplaybook

INITIAL ASSESSMENT DATA COLLECTION

Once teams establish a clear picture of what students need to learn and be able to do, the next step is identifying the learners' current performance levels. We can do this through analyzing a variety of student outcome data from formal assessments, benchmark assessments, student interviews, tests, quizzes and/or activities, and student voice or observation data. It is important to use a variety of data points for analysis. This is often referred to as triangulating data.

When a PLC+ triangulates data they are using multiple forms of overlapping, diverse pieces of evidence and perspectives about student learning to inform their instructional inferences and actions moving forward. Evidence is used from three different sources: conversations with students, observations of student learning, and student products. Conversational evidence is more informal and is used to *know* who the student is as well as gain insight into their vocabulary and language abilities. Observational evidence is gained as the teacher watches and notes how students interact with learning and each other during individual, paired, group, or whole class activities. Product evidence includes evidence more focused on outcomes, such as tests or projects that were used to assess student learning. By using multiple forms of evidence and perspectives, a truer portrait of the student can be developed (Wiggins, 1998).

Your *purpose* should drive your decisions about the type of information and evidence to collect. What is it that students need to learn, and how will you know they have learned it? Several general types of data are especially useful for uncovering academic and nonacademic information about students:

- Analysis of recent student work samples
- Short interviews with a representative sample of students
- Recent initial and end-of-unit assessment results
- Student feedback about a recently completed unit of study

Soliciting Feedback From Your Students

Gathering this type of feedback can be incredibly powerful in better understanding student perceptions of learning. Following is a sample student survey that teachers can use to solicit student feedback about how they feel as learners in the class. You should gather this anonymously, of course. It is important that you use it in a growth-producing manner.

SAMPLE STUDENT FEEDBACK SURVEY

	ALL OF THE TIME	MOST OF THE TIME	SOME OF THE TIME	NONE OF THE TIME
1. My teacher thinks about me as a learner when he or she is planning our lessons.				
2. I am valued as a learner in this class.				
3. I am encouraged to learn new things in this classroom.				
4. I am respected as a learner in this class.				
5. All students are treated the same way in my class.				
6. My teacher finds ways for everyone in class to participate.				

TEAM TIME DISCUSSION

Use the sample student feedback survey as a launching point for discussion about possible ways your team might solicit student feedback.

QUESTION	MY THOUGHTS	OUR COLLECTIVE THOUGHTS
Do we have tools for soliciting student feedback? If so, how are we currently using them?		
What might be the value to us in soliciting feedback from our students?		
What questions might we ask them?		
What errors do we need to avoid? (e.g., maintaining confidentiality)		

TEAM TIME DISCUSSION

Discuss access to current data, and determine how data are currently shared. In what ways can you strengthen your procedures?

QUESTION	WHAT DOES OUR TEAM CURRENTLY DO?	HOW CAN OUR TEAM STRENGTHEN WHAT WE DO MOVING FORWARD?
What assessments of prior student learning does our team currently have access to?		
How does our team gather information to determine what students already know?		
How does our team collect information on student strengths to build upon?		
How does our team collect information to determine what areas of learning need improvement?		
What role does student voice play, or do school climate data play, in the information analyzed?		

STRENGTHS AND OPPORTUNITIES

What strengths does our team currently have in regard to data collection and analysis?		
What opportunities does our team currently have in data collection and analysis?		
What additional information does our team need to determine current student performance levels?		

TEAM TIME DISCUSSION

Use these questions to reach decisions about conceptual and procedural issues for gathering data. You should not feel restricted to the choices listed here.

WHAT IS OUR PURPOSE FOR GATHERING THESE DATA?	• To aid in planning a future unit of study • To get feedback from students about a past unit • To find out about a nonacademic or social and emotional learning indicator • Other
WHAT IS THE SCOPE OF THE DATA COLLECTION?	• Entire class/grade level • Representative sample • Targeted students
WHAT ARE THE CHARACTERISTICS OF THE TIME FRAME WHEN THE DATA WILL BE COLLECTED?	• Specific date, week, or month • Periodically, until improvement is seen
WHAT DATA SOURCE(S) WILL HELP US ANSWER OUR QUESTION ABOUT CURRENT LEVELS OF STUDENT PERFORMANCE?	• Student work samples • Performance data results (standards based) • Performance data results (classroom based) • Survey • Interview • Other

DATA GATHERING

Depending on the results of your team time discussions, you are likely to need additional time for gathering the data. If the data needed are not immediately available, develop a list of tasks so that the data will be made available for the next meeting. Be sure to charge specific team members with gathering the data the team members agreed they needed.

DATA NEEDED	WHO WILL GATHER IT	DATE NEEDED

Preparing for the Data Analysis Protocol

How will the data be assembled and shared with the team?

Ensuring Equity in Data Collection and Analysis

Before the next team meeting, reread "Addressing Bias in Data Collection and Analysis" on pages 73–77 of the companion book *PLC+: Better Decisions and Greater Impact by Design*. Keep these types of implicit biases in mind as you gather data, and in preparation for the group's analysis.

PERSONAL REFLECTION

What types of implicit bias are new to you? How will you be mindful of combatting implicit bias?

Module 8
WHERE ARE WE NOW?
Data Analysis,
Common Challenges,
and Misconception Analysis

PUT THE PLAYBOOK TO WORK FOR YOU

This module spotlights data analysis and identifying a common challenge your team will investigate. Using the data gathered since the last time you met, you will analyze the findings using a protocol designed to assist the group in drawing initial conclusions. A second protocol leads the team through a process for identifying the common challenge, which is the agreed-upon problem of practice for this investigation. The data analysis and common challenge protocols can be used to assist an individual teacher who is seeking support from the team, or by the team as a whole. For the purposes of the Playbook, we focus on a common challenge of the team; these processes are easily adapted to support an individual team member.

As part of the common challenge protocol, you are encouraged to develop or identify a common assessment that will be used to analyze your teaching impact. Detailed instructions for doing so are in Module 17 on page 115. Finally, Module 8 includes a protocol for identifying misconceptions that students have, or are likely to have, that may prevent them from learning the content. This module is likely to be completed over several sessions.

◄ **VIDEO 9: MODULE 8 INTRODUCTION**
resources.corwin.com/plcplaybook

DATA ANALYSIS PROTOCOL

Once your team has a sufficient amount of data, the next step requires an analysis of the data to determine potential steps to move forward. A protocol can serve as a powerful resource in keeping the team focused and efficient during data analysis. It is easy and tempting at times to digress into topics that are not going to impact student growth and achievement. Using a protocol is a way to avoid these diversions while maintaining a structure that supports the intended purpose of the analysis. Take a moment to review the protocol provided below, which is adapted from the National School Reform Faculty.

PROTOCOL FOR EXAMINING DATA

Suggested Time: 45 minutes

Purpose: This protocol is for use in guiding a group through analysis of data to identify strengths and common challenges.

Materials: Copies of data for team members, highlighters, chart paper, note-taking guide on page 66

The activator for this protocol keeps the process moving forward. Any team member can be an activator, who is an active stakeholder and participant in the process.

Checklist to Support Activation

____ Multiple forms of data are used
____ Evidence and research inform decisions

Sample Questions to Support Activation

- How have we used multiple forms of data today to drive our decisions?
- What evidence-based research impacted our decision making?
- What might be other factors that could be impacting the data?
- How do these data affirm what we currently think?
- How do these data disrupt what we currently think and why?

Sample Sentence Starters to Support Activation

- These data are different than what I originally thought because . . .
- A possible cause the data show is . . .
- An evidence-based practice we can think about is . . .

Getting Started: Overview of Data (3 minutes)

The activator for this activity reminds the group of the norms (page 37), assigns roles (recorder, time keeper), and explains the protocol. The activator gives a brief description of the particular data to be discussed and answers clarifying questions as necessary.

Step 1: What parts of these data catch your attention? Just the facts (10 minutes): 2 minutes silently writing individual observations, 8 minutes discussing as a group.

Step 2: What do the data tell us? What do the data *not* tell us? (10 minutes): 3 minutes silently making notes, 7 minutes discussing as a group. Make inferences about the data. *The activator encourages team members to support their statements with evidence from the data.*

Step 3: What good news is there to celebrate? (5 minutes to identify strengths). *The activator asks the group to look for indications of success in the data.*

Step 4: What are possible common challenges suggested by the data? (10 minutes): 3 minutes silently writing individual ideas for practice, 7 minutes discussing as a group. *The activator helps the group narrow the list of possible common challenges to no more than three.*

Step 5: What are our key conclusions? (5 minutes): Identify who will present each of the common challenges in the next protocol. This sets up the next protocol, which is for agreeing on a common challenge for the team.

Source: Adapted from National School Reform Faculty materials.

POSSIBLE COMMON CHALLENGES	PRESENTER
•	
•	
•	

MY NOTES FOR DATA ANALYSIS PROTOCOL

QUESTION	MY THOUGHTS	OUR COLLECTIVE THOUGHTS
Step 1: What parts of these data catch our attention? Just the facts.		
Step 2: What do the data tell us? What do the data *not* tell us?		
Step 3: What good news is there to celebrate?		
Step 4: What are possible common challenges suggested by the data?		
Step 5: What are our key conclusions?		

COMMON CHALLENGE PROTOCOL

Now that there is an understanding of where you are going (first guiding question: "Where are we going?") and of current student proficiency levels, areas of strength, and places for improvement (second guiding question: "Where are we now?"), your team can identify a common challenge. The common challenge is the team's agreed-upon problem of practice, and it drives the work of the PLC+ team. Use the quality checklist below to monitor the development of the common challenge to be investigated.

COMMON CHALLENGE QUALITY CHECKLIST

☐ Is the common challenge grounded in the data we gathered during the "Where are we now?" phase?

☐ Is the common challenge observable and actionable?

☐ Will addressing the common challenge make a significant difference in students' learning?

☐ Is the common challenge something that the team is curious about?

☐ Does the common challenge mobilize and motivate the PLC+ team to engage in the work?

Once the PLC+ team has developed a quality common challenge, effective and efficient progress toward addressing that common challenge requires the team to fine-tune their work together. This tuning process helps avoid common challenges that are too vague or too broad, that have too much packed into a single challenge, or that are related to something outside the limits of the PLC+ team.

COMMON CHALLENGE TUNING PROTOCOL

Suggested Time: Up to 25 minutes per possible common challenge

Purpose: There are times when the PLC+ team as a whole will share a common challenge, and other times where an individual team member is looking for the support of his or her colleagues. The following protocol can be used to explore the common challenge at both levels.

Materials: The activator will need to gather or delegate the gathering of all materials necessary for engaging in this process.

Getting Started: Identify an activator for this protocol, and assign a time keeper and, if desired, a recorder. Because the activator is assisting the team in moving the discussion forward, we advise that the activator not simultaneously serve as a presenter. Another activator can assume the role for him or her during that time.

Step 1: Presenter shares common challenge and describes (5 minutes):

- Where it came from—who was involved in identifying it and its connection to data

- Context of other school or district efforts to address problem

Step 2: Team members ask factual clarifying questions (5 minutes)

Step 3: Presenter steps back (remains silent 8–10 minutes) while team members provide

- *Warm feedback:* aspects of the common challenge that (based on the criteria and list of potential challenges) make them think this will work well to address student needs

- *Cool feedback:* concerns or questions about the common challenge, including tuning suggestions

- *Stretches:* other things the presenter may not have thought about, but that might support the goals of the PLC+

Step 4: Presenter rejoins for general discussion (balance of 25 minutes' time), including

- Responses and factual clarifications by presenter

- Feedback from team members focused on supporting the common challenge and not to be taken personally; it is not an evaluation of an individual teacher, but rather a collective brainstorm to respond to the common challenge

- Reflections by all participants about what they learned

Step 5: Repeat the common challenge protocol to discuss the next proposed challenge.

NOTES

_____

_____

_____

_____

_____

_____

_____

_____

REACHING CONSENSUS ON THE COMMON CHALLENGE

Once all of the possible common challenges have been discussed, it is time to reach agreement on the one that will drive the team's inquiry cycle.

Step 1: Consider the possible common challenges.

- What are the relative strengths of and barriers to each?
- How does each possible challenge rate on the common challenge quality checklist on page 67?

Step 2: Propose a common challenge.

- Members formulate a proposed common challenge, amending it to reflect discussion.
- Members work together to solve problems and to tune the proposed common challenge.
- Test for agreement:
  - I will fully support our inquiry cycle investigating this common challenge.
  - I am in support of my colleagues' decision.
  - I will not block this decision.

The activator asks, "Are there any further questions or concerns about the common challenge we have selected?" If there is no further discussion, then agreement has been reached. If there is a call of concern, the person raising the concern reexamines by repeating Steps 1 and 2.

Step 3: Debrief the protocol.

- Plus/delta on the protocol itself: What did the group do well? What could have been improved? Make notes about refinements for future processes for the common challenge protocol.

OUR COMMON CHALLENGE FOR THIS INQUIRY CYCLE IS

DATE

NOTES FOR REFINING FUTURE COMMON CHALLENGE PROTOCOL

Step 4: Plan for development of a common assessment.

Now that you have identified your common challenge, you might develop or adopt a common assessment that will be used as an initial assessment and as a postassessment. Sometimes teams create their own common assessments, and other times there are tools available that can be used for this purpose. Common assessment data allow you to gauge the impact of your teaching and monitor the progress and achievement of students. Detailed directions for developing a common assessment are in Module 17 on page 115. Common assessment development takes time, and your team will likely want to schedule a separate session to do so. However, it is advisable to schedule this before ending the meeting.

PLANS TO DEVELOP A COMMON ASSESSMENT
(OR ENSURE CURRENT COMMON ASSESSMENT GATHERS
EVIDENCE RELATED TO OUR COMMON CHALLENGE)

DATE, TIME, AND LOCATION

MATERIALS NEEDED

Source: Adapted from material in *Instructional Rounds in Education: A Network Approach to Improving Teaching and Learning,* by E. City, R. Elmore, S. Fiarman, & L. Teitel (Harvard Education Press, 2009).

IDENTIFY STUDENT MISCONCEPTIONS

One way a team supports student learning is through identifying student misconceptions and intentionally teaching toward them. This can be done prior to engaging in instruction or after evidence has been collected. When it is done prior to instruction, teams think about where potential student misconceptions may lie, and they develop proactive instructional responses to address these misconceptions head on. Teams can use data from prior units completed with current students, or they can use trend data from when the unit was previously taught. The strength in doing this prior to instruction is that possible instructional responses and strategies to support learning are already identified. This allows for teacher response to be focused and immediate.

While it is fully recognized that not every potential misconception can be identified for every learner, identifying common patterns strengthens the impact teachers can have on improving the growth and achievement of students. Teams can also engage in identifying student misconceptions after data have been collected. This allows PLC+ teams to become diagnostic in regard to current gaps in learning, and develop appropriate instructional responses moving forward.

A sixth-grade team used their common challenge to identify misconceptions and then determine possible instructional responses. The following table summarizes the conversation that they had about misconceptions and their responses to those misconceptions.

Common Challenge: Initial assessment results show that students struggle with connecting textual evidence to inferences.

COMMON STUDENT MISCONCEPTIONS	INSTRUCTIONAL RESPONSE	POSSIBLE STRATEGIES
Students interpret text too literally.	Students who have this misconception need practice and support taking the evidence they are able to explicitly identify and use it to make accurate inferences about the text.	Use visuals (e.g., panels in a graphic novel) so students understand how explicit details support making inferences. Model this first, and then couple the model with whole group guided instruction and collaborative learning. Provide students with interpretive prompts to think about their explicit key details to draw inferences (e.g., "How did you arrive at that conclusion?" "What is the author's point of view, and how do you know?")

(Continued)

(Continued)

COMMON STUDENT MISCONCEPTIONS	INSTRUCTIONAL RESPONSE	POSSIBLE STRATEGIES
Students look for a single main idea in the first or last lines of text. They fail to recognize that middle school readings are more sophisticated and rarely use this simple organizational structure.	Students who have this misconception need practice and support synthesizing textual evidence that is presented throughout the text.	Provide students with a note-taking device that has them paraphrase each paragraph and enumerate textual evidence.
Students read too quickly and miss important textual evidence.	Students who have this misconception need practice in reading closely so that they can locate evidence.	Provide students with close reading instruction, and build their annotation skills

Common Challenge

COMMON STUDENT MISCONCEPTIONS	INSTRUCTIONAL RESPONSE	POSSIBLE STRATEGIES

Module 9

WHERE ARE WE NOW?
Crosscutting Values Check

PUT THE PLAYBOOK TO WORK FOR YOU

The purpose of this module is to revisit the crosscutting values of the PLC+ framework and determine the ways in which they are realized in your work. The crosscutting values check allows teams to make adjustments to improve learning for students and teachers. We revisit these values toward the end of each major PLC+ question.

EQUITY AND EXPECTATIONS VALUES CHECKLIST

The core values of the PLC+ framework include equity and expectations. Without these values, student learning varies considerably, and often students are blamed for their lack of progress or achievement. Members of a PLC+ team assume responsibility for the learning of all students and are willing to talk honestly, and openly, about how they can best meet the needs of all of their students. When we directly discuss the values of equity and expectations, we may uncover assumptions that need to be addressed. The following checklist provides some questions that PLC+ teams have found useful in checking in on their values.

◀ **VIDEO 10: MODULE 9 INTRODUCTION**
resources.corwin.com/plcplaybook

QUESTION	MY THOUGHTS	OUR COLLECTIVE THOUGHTS
Did we collect initial assessment data?		
Did we identify strengths as well as needs?		
Do we understand students' cultural backgrounds and the knowledge and experiences they bring to the classroom? Are we using this information in our instruction?		
Did we analyze the data to identify patterns and trends? What did we learn?		
Did we analyze the initial assessment data such that we could make decisions about what *not* to teach?		
Do we have a common challenge that will guide our work moving forward? If not, why? (Have we missed a specific need of our students to focus our efforts and passions?)		

ACTIVATE LEARNING FOR MYSELF AND OTHERS CHECKLIST

Student learning needs drive adult learning needs. Once teams understand where students are now in their learning journey, teams need to take a step back to reflect on their personal learning. Are there any adult learning needs that must be met to best be able to support student learning? As already discussed, the + in the PLC+ is you, and so it is important to recognize learning for teachers is a constant. Based on the trend data and the common challenge, what learning do you (or your team) need to accomplish to ensure that all students are successful?

WHAT ARE THE ADULT LEARNING IMPLICATIONS OF THE COMMON CHALLENGE?	WHAT ARE MY LEARNING NEEDS SO I CAN MEET MY STUDENTS' LEARNING NEEDS? What strategies might I need to learn more about?	WHAT LEARNING WILL I ENGAGE IN TO MEET MY LEARNING NEEDS? What will I do on my own? What can I do with colleagues?

COLLECTIVE EFFICACY CHECKLIST

Teams that are empowered to make decisions, act, communicate clearly, and hold themselves accountable for their efforts manifest high degrees of collective teacher efficacy (CTE). Use the table below to gauge and monitor the actions that will follow your work about the second guiding question, "Where are we now?"

QUESTION	MY THOUGHTS	OUR COLLECTIVE THOUGHTS
In what ways has the data collection and analysis process impacted us? Have we been challenged by what we have found?		
Do we feel confident that collectively we can meet the needs of our students?		
How will we support the decisions our team has made?		
How might the common challenge change our collective work?		

Module 10

GUIDING QUESTION 3: HOW DO WE MOVE LEARNING FORWARD?

Strengthening Our Teaching Practices

PUT THE PLAYBOOK TO WORK FOR YOU

These next five modules (10–14) focus on the guiding question "How do we move learning forward?" Too often, professional learning communities are data rich yet information poor. This question gets at the heart of the PLC+ process—*teaching and impacting learning*. The modules in this section equip teams with a means for using evidence of student learning and effective teaching, and designing learning tasks for students to move them forward in their learning. Unlike those in previous sections, these modules are not linear. Rather, they are tools your team can use as needed, as often as is needed, and in any order, depending on the needs of the team.

PLC+ Framework Guiding Questions

1. **Where are we going?**
2. **Where are we now?**
3. **How do we move learning forward?**
4. **What did we learn today?**
5. **Who benefited and who did not benefit?**

◀ **VIDEO 11: MODULE 10 INTRODUCTION**
resources.corwin.com/plcplaybook

PAIR TEACHING STRATEGIES WITH EVIDENCE GATHERING

Teaching strategies abound, but not all have a strong research base behind them. As one example, the practice of teaching to "learning styles" (visual, auditory, and kinesthetic) has no research base, yet remains popular in some quarters (Pasquinelli, 2012). Teachers need comprehensive resources that report on the effectiveness of strategies, so they can make evidence-informed instructional responses about what, when, and with whom to use approaches. Two such comprehensive resources that are easily accessible are John Hattie's Visible Learning research and the U.S. Department of Education's What Works Clearinghouse (https://ies.ed.gov/ncee/wwc).

Consider the common challenge your team has identified. What research-based instructional strategies might be well suited for this purpose? Once the PLC+ has agreed upon a few universal strategies to try, discuss the evidence-gathering method you will use as well to monitor your impact on student learning. Although your team need not be completely lock step in instruction, you will want to agree upon some universal evidence-gathering methods to support a collaborative analysis of the impact of your instructional decisions, and to formatively assess in order to make timely instructional adjustments.

As an example, recall the third-grade team who analyzed a standard and developed learning progressions, learning intentions, and success criteria in Module 5. They identified a common challenge and worked through identifying instructional responses and corresponding evidence-gathering methods to monitor implementation and gauge impact. Importantly, this conversation provided the team with the opportunity to adjust instruction before the end of the unit. Keep in mind that assessment is assessment. Whether it is to be used formatively (e.g., to make instructional adjustments) is a measure of the sophistication of a team. To relegate assessment to a summative function only (e.g., awarding grades) is a lost opportunity. In agreeing on the evidence they would gather and analyze, this third-grade team made it possible to formatively assess and adjust instruction.

NOTES

_____

_____

_____

_____

_____

_____

_____

THIRD-GRADE EXAMPLE FOR MAIN IDEAS AND KEY DETAILS

Common Challenge: Initial assessment results show that students struggle with connecting key details in informational texts to determine the main idea.

EVIDENCE-INFORMED INSTRUCTIONAL RESPONSE

1. Teacher Modeling: Teachers will model the process of looking at key details found in a piece of text and make connections between them to determine the main idea.

2. Student Think-Alouds: Using think-alouds will allow teachers to gather evidence on how students are processing their key details and making meaning of them. This will provide teachers with insight into where and why student gaps are present as well as create a baseline to measure growth moving forward.

3. Graphic Organizers: Graphic organizers will support and guide students in understanding how to appropriately collect and process key information in a text.

EVIDENCE-GATHERING METHODS

1. Observation data from student think-alouds, with targeted look-fors to support expert noticing

2. Students will complete a three-column graphic organizer to record key details, and provide an explanation of their key detail and overall synthesis.

3. Students will answer an extended-response question asking them to use key details they collected and identify the main idea of the text.

NOTES

_____

_____

_____

_____

_____

_____

_____

_____

_____

TEAM TIME DISCUSSION

Use the template below to make decisions about some universally used instructional practices to target the common challenge you identified.

Common Challenge

EVIDENCE-INFORMED INSTRUCTIONAL RESPONSE	EVIDENCE-GATHERING METHOD

COACHING CORNERS PROTOCOL

Suggested Time: 20–30 minutes

Purpose: Research-based evidence about instructional strategies is coupled with the expertise within the team. However, knowledge may be distributed differently across the team. Coaching is provided to a small group of colleagues before implementation. Anyone on the team can be a coach; years of experience and expertise are not one and the same. Team members demonstrating a strategy or technique are always volunteers. Use coaching corners to demonstrate and teach a specific strategy or technique to your team. Use the protocol below to build one another's pedagogical content knowledge.

Materials: The activator for Coaching Corners should gather or delegate the gathering of materials for demonstrating the strategies or techniques.

Step 1: Introduce the strategy or technique: Provide background information about the approach, justification/evidence of effectiveness (both personally and in the research base), and any relevant data.

Step 2: Outline the strategy: Consistently using a new practice requires developing specific knowledge, skills, and dispositions. The activator could add the following questions to deepen the learning:

- How is this strategy different than what we are already doing?
- What is about this strategy that leads us to believe it will facilitate learning?
- What is essential to understand about this strategy to implement it?
- What are the basic steps?
- How do you implement it?
- In what context will it be used? (e.g., when introducing content, during small group instruction)
- What are the pitfalls to avoid?

Step 3: Practice session: Lead peers through the identified strategy, or use a short video of yourself implementing it with students. Provide materials used with students, and give time for participants to rehearse the strategy. The practice session should be no more than 10 minutes in length.

Step 4: Feedback and clarifying questions: The "coach" for the session and the "students" provide feedback about the strategy that is helpful, positive, and specific. The discussion should include opportunities to ask and respond to clarifying questions. In addition, discuss opportunities to observe one another enacting the identified instructional strategy.

Step 5: Debrief the coaching corners experience.

WHAT QUESTIONS DO WE STILL HAVE?	
HOW WILL WE OBSERVE ONE ANOTHER IN IMPLEMENTING THIS STRATEGY?	
WHAT ADDITIONAL RESOURCES MIGHT WE UTILIZE TO REFINE OUR KNOWLEDGE OF THIS STRATEGY?	

Module 11

HOW DO WE MOVE LEARNING FORWARD?

Assignment Analysis

PUT THE PLAYBOOK TO WORK FOR YOU

The purpose of this module is to provide teams with a tool to analyze the assignments that are given to students. Answering the question, "How do we move learning forward?" requires that teams develop appropriate tasks for students to complete. Too often, rigor levels are diluted in engineered tasks for students, holding them to a lower expectation than what is appropriate. Educational equity demands that standards and the rigor embedded within them are held constant and expectations remain consistently high, such that opportunities to learn are delivered to all students.

As a team, you will want to analyze some of the assignments you give to students. In doing so, you will identify appropriate levels of rigor and the expectations the team has for students' learning. You will also see if the assignment is designed to provide students access to grade level standards or if the expectations are below grade level.

The tool in this module can be used in a variety of grades and content areas; it is especially appropriate for tasks for which a text is critical. If there is no central text for the assignment, skip the first part of the tool and focus on the remaining sections. The idea is to use the prompts to foster discussion among members of the team. Doing so calibrates expectations among the team and helps ensure that all students have access to rigorous learning experiences. It's important to be honest in these conversations, as agreeing on a low-level task is not going to ensure that students learn at high levels.

◀ **VIDEO 12: MODULE 11 INTRODUCTION**
resources.corwin.com/plcplaybook

ASSIGNMENT ANALYSIS TOOL

Step 1: Determine the Key Features of the Assignment

Text Type (literary, informational, visual, multiple texts)	
Text Length (excerpt, chapter, etc.)	
Text Complexity (quantitative and qualitative values that suggest the grade range of the selected text)	
Writing Output (no writing, note taking, one or two sentences, multiple short responses, one paragraph, multiple paragraphs)	
Length of Assignment (15 minutes or less, one or two class periods, multiple weeks, linked to an ongoing project (quarter/semester/year)	
Student Thinking *Webb's Depth of Knowledge* • Recall and reproduction • Basic application of skills/concepts • Strategic thinking • Extended thinking	

Step 2: Assignment Analysis

1. Alignment With Standards

A standards-aligned assignment has essential features. First and most important, it must be grade-level appropriate. The assignment must embrace instructional shifts, including regular practice with complex texts; academic language; read, write, and speak using evidence; and build knowledge through content information. The assignment is clearly articulated so that students can fully understand what is expected of them.

Assignment Analysis for Alignment With Standards

2. Centrality of Text

The centrality of the text allows students to grapple with key ideas, author's craft and intent, and larger meanings. Students have the opportunity to display increasing expertise in interpreting and responding to text, and to draw evidence from text to justify their responses and thinking. Specifically, an assignment fully reflects this centrality of text when students are required to cite evidence (e.g., paraphrasing, direct citation) to support a position or claim.

Assignment Analysis for Centrality of Text

3. Cognitive Challenge

The cognitive work required to retell a story, identify facts from a text, analyze a character using textual evidence, or apply knowledge gained from multiple texts to form new ideas ranges from simple to complex. Generally, the cognitive challenge increases through text-dependent questions and assignments that require student documentation of their deep analysis or the construction of new knowledge. Use Webb's Depth of Knowledge levels in your analysis. The expectation of an extended written response (multiple paragraphs), which is governed by the acceptable practices of the discipline, most strongly supports such thinking.

Assignment Analysis for Cognitive Challenge

4. Motivation to Engage in Learning

For learners to thrive and achieve at high levels, educators must embrace both the content of the curriculum and the design of instruction. Each of these elements impacts student attention, interest, motivation, and cognitive effort and must be considered in the design of assignments. Specifically, we prioritize choice and relevancy. Students must be given some level of autonomy and independence in their tasks—with rigor maintained across all options. And the tasks must be relevant as they focus on poignant topics, use real-world materials and experiences, and give students the opportunity to make connections with their goals, interests, and values.

Assignment Analysis for Motivation to Engage in Learning

Source: Adapted from *Checking In: Do Classroom Assignments Reflect Today's Higher Standards?* by S. Santelises and J. Dabrowski (The Education Trust, 2015).

TEAM TIME DISCUSSION

Use this space to focus on improving aspects of the assignment that need more attention.

1. **Alignment With Standards**

2. **Centrality of Text**

3. **Cognitive Challenge**

4. **Motivation to Engage in Learning**

Module 12

HOW DO WE MOVE LEARNING FORWARD?

Learning Walks

PUT THE PLAYBOOK TO WORK FOR YOU

High-functioning teams have members who are professionally generous. You will recall that Module 1 spotlighted characteristics of effective professional learning communities. Of particular relevance for this module are the characteristics related to collective learning and peer support (Hord, 2004). These traits are expressed in the routine practice of spending time in each other's classrooms. This module describes procedures for learning walks.

WHAT IS A LEARNING WALK?

Unlike more formal instructional rounds (City, Elmore, Fiarman, & Teitel, 2009), learning walks are more loosely structured. The focus might be on the common challenge or on implementation of a specific instructional strategy. A learning walk might be conducted as a means to talk with students or to examine the physical environment. A learning walk can be conducted within a PLC+ team or across teams. Ultimately, it is the participants themselves that determine the purpose of the walk. Volunteer teachers open their classrooms to these scheduled learning walks. More information on learning walks can be found on pages 106–110 of the companion book *PLC+: Better Decisions and Greater Impact by Design.*

◄ **VIDEO 13: MODULE 12 INTRODUCTION**
resources.corwin.com/plcplaybook

TYPES OF LEARNING WALKS AND THEIR PURPOSES

In every classroom, there are three influences on learning: the teacher, the students, and the classroom environment. Learning walks focus on one or more of these influences and are driven by the purposes determined by the PLC+ team. Each has unique qualities that lend themselves to investigation of teaching and learning.

Ghost walks are the least formal and are excellent for teams to conduct when students are not present. Because teams typically meet face-to-face on early-release days, ghost walks are especially easy to arrange. Team members select a focus for their learning and walk each other's classrooms as a group. An activator selected by the team leads the ghost walk.

Capacity-building learning walks can be used both within and across professional learning communities. Volunteer teachers open up their classrooms for short observations (seven minutes) with a predetermined area of focus. An activator designated by the PLC+ team hosts the learning walk. Observers are divided into three teams (A, B, and C), and have a specific task to conduct in each classroom. The observers debrief after three classroom visits, and the discussion is confined to patterns gleaned; it is not about individual classrooms. The composition of the team rotates so that observers have the experience of collecting data across all three sources (teacher, students, and environment.) A team debrief of the experience is conducted at the end to draw conclusions about implementation and next steps. A sample schedule of a capacity-building learning walk can be found on pages 90–91 in this Playbook.

Faculty learning walks include all the faculty in a school, although all faculty members do not necessarily participate on a single day. The purpose is for other PLC+ teams in the school to demonstrate their practices to colleagues outside of the team to which they belong. Faculty learning walks may be co-led by administrators, the instructional leadership team, and an activator from the designated PLC+ team. Floating substitute teachers might be hired to cover classrooms, or designated planning time might be used. Ideally, these occur twice per school year. A facultywide debrief across PLC+ teams can be held to discuss future professional learning.

NOTES

_____

_____

_____

_____

_____

_____

TYPES OF LEARNING WALKS AND THEIR PURPOSES

TYPE OF WALK	PURPOSE	TIME	PARTICIPANTS	FOLLOW-UP AFTER THE WALK
Ghost Walk	To examine classrooms without students present. Teachers volunteer to make their classrooms available and in turn are participants in the ghost walk. The focus of the observation is the physical learning environment.	Between 30 minutes and 1 hour	Members of the professional learning community	*Summary of data collected:* Evidence and wonderings processed within the PLC+ team, or across other professional learning communities
Capacity-Building Learning Walk	This walk focuses solely on collecting data to inform decisions. Collection of data and evidence help identify the implementation of effective practices and gain insights into next steps.	Between 45 minutes and 2 hours	Members of the building leadership team, in partnership with members of the professional learning communities	*Summary of data collected:* Evidence and wonderings processed within the PLC+ team, or with entire faculty
Faculty Learning Walk	The goal of this type of learning walk is to focus on the learning of the whole staff. It involves all teachers in visiting the classrooms of other teachers outside of the PLC+ to which members belong. This can spark new ideas and strategies for teachers to incorporate into their own practice.	At least half of the day but often the full day	Principal, assistant principal, members of the building leadership team, and whoever is available each period and/or time segment, ultimately involving entire faculty throughout the year	*Summary of data collected:* Evidence and wonderings processed with entire faculty

CAPACITY-BUILDING LEARNING WALK

Suggested Time: 2 hours

Purpose: To collect observational data about an agreed-upon focus, in order to assist our PLC+ team in gaining insight into implementation, and to make decisions about our next steps.

Focus: We are examining _____

SCHEDULE (No more than 7 minutes per class)	WHAT IS THE *TEACHER* DOING? Team A	HOW DO *STUDENTS* DESCRIBE THEIR LEARNING? Team B	HOW DOES THE *ENVIRONMENT* SUPPORT THE LEARNING? Team C
Classroom 1: Time:			
Classroom 2: Time:			
Classroom 3: Time:			

ROUND 1 DEBRIEF OF CLASSROOMS 1-3: WHAT PATTERNS DID WE NOTICE IN EACH OF THESE THREE AREAS?

SCHEDULE (No more than 7 minutes per class)	WHAT IS THE *TEACHER* DOING? Team B	HOW DO *STUDENTS* DESCRIBE THEIR LEARNING? Team C	HOW DOES THE *ENVIRONMENT* SUPPORT THE LEARNING? Team A
Classroom 4: Time:			
Classroom 5: Time:			

SCHEDULE (No more than 7 minutes per class)	WHAT IS THE *TEACHER* DOING? Team B	HOW DO *STUDENTS* DESCRIBE THEIR LEARNING? Team C	HOW DOES THE *ENVIRONMENT* SUPPORT THE LEARNING? Team A
Classroom 6: Time:			

ROUND 2 DEBRIEF OF CLASSROOMS 4-6: WHAT PATTERNS DID WE NOTICE IN EACH OF THESE THREE AREAS?

SCHEDULE (No more than 7 minutes per class)	WHAT IS THE *TEACHER* DOING? Team C	HOW DO *STUDENTS* DESCRIBE THEIR LEARNING? Team A	HOW DOES THE *ENVIRONMENT* SUPPORT THE LEARNING? Team B
Classroom 7: Time:			
Classroom 8: Time:			
Classroom 9: Time:			

ROUND 3 DEBRIEF OF CLASSROOMS 7-9: WHAT PATTERNS DID WE NOTICE IN EACH OF THESE THREE AREAS?

CAPACITY-BUILDING LEARNING WALK DEBRIEFING NOTES

Focus: We are examining _____

ROUND 1 DEBRIEF: PATTERNED OBSERVATIONS OF TEAMS A, B, AND C
(9 minutes)

Team A reports on what the *teachers* were doing.	Team B reports on how *students* described their learning.	Team C reports on the ways in which the *environment* supported the learning.

ROUND 2 DEBRIEF: PATTERNED OBSERVATIONS OF TEAMS B, C, AND A
(9 minutes)

Team B reports on what the *teachers* were doing.	Team C reports on how *students* described their learning.	Team A reports on the ways in which the *environment* supported the learning.

ROUND 3 DEBRIEF: PATTERNED OBSERVATIONS OF TEAMS C, A, AND B
(9 minutes)

Team C reports on what the *teachers* were doing.	Team A reports on how *students* described their learning.	Team B reports on the ways in which the *environment* supported the learning.

OVERALL DEBRIEF OF THE EXPERIENCE (20 minutes)

What conclusions can we reach about implementation?

What conclusions can we reach about strengths?

What conclusions can we reach about opportunities for growth as a team?

How might we refine this process for future capacity-building learning walks?

TEAM TIME DISCUSSION

QUESTION	MY THOUGHTS	OUR COLLECTIVE THOUGHTS
What is the value to our collective efforts in conducting learning walks?		
How can learning walks develop our individual and collective efficacy?		
What are some important considerations to think about when considering learning walks to strengthen our team?		
Where might be an entry point for our PLC+ to begin exploring learning walks?		

(Continued)

(Continued)

OUR NEXT LEARNING WALK WILL BE . . . (TYPE AND DATE)	DESIGNATED ACTIVATOR FOR THE LEARNING WALK	PRELIMINARY LOGISTICS (DETAILS TO FOLLOW FROM ACTIVATOR)

Module 13

HOW DO WE MOVE LEARNING FORWARD?
Microteaching

PUT THE PLAYBOOK TO WORK FOR YOU

The heartbeat of a PLC+ rests on the quality time members invest in one another engaged in inquiry of their practices. Time spent in each other's classrooms is an essential part of this equation. However, the logistics of teaching limit the opportunities educators have to conduct learning walks. Microteaching is another way to bring your team members into your classroom digitally. As with the other modules in this section, microteaching can be utilized at any point in your work as a professional learning community. In fact, we encourage its frequent and regular use as an effective means for leveraging the collective strength of your team and for regular feedback on the implementation of new practices.

MICROTEACHING IN A PROFESSIONAL LEARNING COMMUNITY

Microteaching is a teacher-directed coaching process that uses video recording as a platform for discussion. Hattie (2012) reports that meta-analyses of microteaching have yielded an effect size of 0.88, more than doubling the acceleration of student learning during one year of time. This is with good reason, as microteaching equips educators with a tool for asking questions that mediate the thinking of the teacher. More information on microteaching can be found on pages 110–113 in the companion book *PLC+: Better Decisions and Greater Impact by Design*.

◀ **VIDEO 14: MODULE 13 INTRODUCTION**
resources.corwin.com/plcplaybook

The process is a relatively simple one. The volunteer teacher determines a teaching practice for discussion. In the case of the PLC+, this is likely to focus on the identified common challenge of the current inquiry cycle, or an instructional strategy the team is working toward. The teacher arranges to be video-recorded for part of a lesson, either with assistance from another adult, or utilizing self-recording technology. The teacher then views the recording individually and isolates a segment for discussion with team colleagues. The teacher explains the context of the video to the team and poses his or her question. The team then watches the video segment selected by the teacher. The discussion that follows is important, both in terms of what it is and what it is not.

WHAT MICROTEACHING IS		WHAT MICROTEACHING IS NOT
To co-construct content pedagogical knowledge with the team	**Purpose**	To evaluate someone else's teaching
Identified by the teacher	**Determination of Focus**	Identified by others
Directs the discussion	**Role of the Teacher**	Listens passively
To ask mediating questions to prompt the thinking of the teacher	**Role of Other PLC+ Members**	To provide feedback about the quality of the lesson, to offer judgments and personal opinions

PREPARATION FOR MICROTEACHING: THE VOLUNTEER TEACHER

BEFORE FILMING

What are your goals for this process (e.g., to improve a teaching technique, to refine your ability to engage in expert noticing, to identify the thinking of a student)?

When and with whom will you need to schedule filming? Who will you need for assistance before, during, or after filming?

What equipment will you need?

What do you hope to capture in the video? What specifically do you hope to see from your students? What aspects of their learning do you hope will progress and move forward?

AFTER FILMING

Schedule time to review the footage.

In what ways was the lesson you delivered different from the lesson you planned?

What questions does the video raise for you? What did you see from your students that raised those questions?

(Continued)

(Continued)

(Continued)

AFTER FILMING

What questions do you want your team to help you answer?

IN YOUR PLC+ TEAM MEETING

Introduce the video to your team, set the context, and pose your major questions.

Suggested team member questions:

- What did you want your students to know and be able to do?
- What connections have you made?
- What did you see or hear that confirms your previous thinking?
- What did you see or hear that conflicts with your previous thinking?
- Which moments did you find to be particularly effective?
- Which moments did you think did not go as well as you had hoped?
- What was different in comparing those moments?
- What would you change in order to accomplish your stated goal?
- What do you want to be sure to do again?

DEBRIEF THE MICROTEACHING EXPERIENCE AS A WHOLE

What did we learn today as a team?

How might we move student learning forward?

How might we move our own learning forward?

What goals do we have for ourselves for the next two weeks?

Module 14

HOW DO WE MOVE LEARNING FORWARD?
Crosscutting Values Check

PUT THE PLAYBOOK TO WORK FOR YOU

The purpose of this module is to revisit the crosscutting values of the PLC+ framework and determine the ways in which they are realized in your work. The crosscutting values check allows teams to make adjustments to improve learning for students and teachers.

Equity

High Expectations

Individual and Collective Efficacy

Activation

◄ **VIDEO 15: MODULE 14 INTRODUCTION**
resources.corwin.com/plcplaybook

EQUITY AND EXPECTATIONS VALUES CHECKLIST

The core values of the PLC+ framework include equity and expectations. Without these values, student learning varies considerably, and often students are blamed for their lack of progress or achievement. Members of a PLC+ team assume responsibility for the learning of all students and are willing to talk honestly, and openly, about how they can best meet the needs of all of their students. When we directly discuss the values of equity and expectations, we may uncover assumptions that need to be addressed. The following checklist provides some questions that PLC+ teams have found useful in checking in on their values.

QUESTION	MY THOUGHTS	OUR COLLECTIVE THOUGHTS
Did we consider the best evidence for the instructional approaches we discussed?		
Did we analyze assignments for their appropriateness?		
Did we provide compensatory and adaptive supports for students who needed them?		
Do we overscaffold for some students because we believe that they cannot achieve at the same level as other students?		
Did we discuss our visits to each other's classrooms with a focus on teaching *and* learning?		
Have we agreed to video-record our instruction and talk with peers about improving both teaching *and* learning?		
Do we have a plan that will allow us to address the common challenge?		

ACTIVATE LEARNING FOR MYSELF AND OTHERS CHECKLIST

Student learning needs drive adult learning needs. Once teams understand where students are now in their learning journey, teams need to take a step back to reflect on their personal learning. Are there any adult learning needs that must be met to best be able to support student learning? As already discussed, the + in the PLC+ is you, and so it is important to recognize learning for teachers is a constant. Given that you want to move student learning forward, what learning do you (or your team) need to accomplish to ensure that all students are successful?

WHAT DID WE DECIDE TO DO TO MOVE STUDENT LEARNING FORWARD?	WHAT ARE MY LEARNING NEEDS SO I CAN MEET MY STUDENTS' LEARNING NEEDS? What strategies might I need to learn more about?	WHAT LEARNING WILL I ENGAGE IN TO MEET MY LEARNING NEEDS? What will I do on my own? What can I do with colleagues?

COLLECTIVE EFFICACY CHECKLIST

Teams that are empowered to make decisions, act, communicate clearly, and hold themselves accountable for their efforts manifest high degrees of collective teacher efficacy (CTE). Use the checklist below to gauge and monitor the actions that will follow your work about the third question, "How do we move learning forward?"

QUESTION	MY THOUGHTS	OUR COLLECTIVE THOUGHTS
How confident are we in the evidence used to select instructional strategies?		
What data will we collect that demonstrate success for the team?		
Do we believe we have the skills and knowledge necessary to implement the strategies we have identified?		
Do all of our team members feel supported as they try new strategies and approaches?		

Module 15
GUIDING QUESTION 4: WHAT DID WE LEARN TODAY?

PUT THE PLAYBOOK TO WORK FOR YOU

Modules 15–19 of the Playbook focus on the PLC+ guiding question "What did we learn today?" Actions sparked by the team's inquiry generate data that need to be analyzed to determine impact. Yet too often, evidence of student learning is discussed superficially, confining discussion only to identifying students who made progress (or did not). Rarely is there an intentional reflection on the learning that took place within the PLC+ that will in turn support accelerating student learning in the classroom. The purpose of this module is to foster your team's examination of student learning and your own learning such that changes can be made to the learning environment. Intentional discussions about what we learned allow teachers to build their evaluation skills and to use assessment data formatively.

PLC+ Framework Guiding Questions

1. **Where are we going?**

2. **Where are we now?**

3. **How do we move learning forward?**

4. **What did we learn today?**

5. **Who benefited and who did not benefit?**

◄ **VIDEO 16: MODULE 15 INTRODUCTION**
resources.corwin.com/plcplaybook

BUILD THE HABIT OF REFLECTION

"What did *we* learn today?" That is a core question every PLC+ should ask during their collaboration experiences, whether they are participating in face-to-face meetings, professional learning, or learning walks. This should occur for many reasons, but mostly because teachers above all else have one thing in common: They are *time-impoverished.* Time is the most precious resource teachers have, and coming together to collaborate about teaching and learning is an investment of precious time. Teachers abhor any time-wasting activities, and their professional learning community time is limited. Educators come together to become better at their craft and learn new methodologies, strategies, and approaches to teaching. The PLC+ framework is designed to link organizational learning to current actions intended to increase student learning. A simple question we should ask ourselves is: *What did we just learn?* If we didn't learn anything, we have to ask ourselves one profound question: *Why did we meet?*

You will recall the third-grade team introduced in Module 5 who were teaching their students about linking key details to main ideas in informational texts. At the end of one meeting midway through the unit, they engaged in extended collaborative reflection about the early results of their instruction.

NOTES

_____

_____

_____

_____

_____

_____

_____

_____

_____

_____

_____

_____

_____

_____

_____

THIRD-GRADE REFLECTION EXAMPLE

QUESTION	OUR COLLECTIVE REFLECTIONS
What was our focus of the meeting? Did we keep our dialogue and discussion primarily concentrated on the main focus of the meeting?	To determine how our students are progressing in mastery related to standard RI.3.2 ELA-Literacy RI.3.2: Determine the main idea of a text; recount the key details and explain how they support the main idea.
What evidence did we examine?	We examined assessment results for how well our students were able to recount key details and link them to a main idea.
What did the evidence tell us about student learning and our teaching?	We found that most of our students could name details, but they still struggled in their ability to make judgments about what was <u>key</u> vs. what was <u>interesting</u>. They also struggled with using the key details to identify the main idea. We realized that we hadn't really modeled how we make decisions like this to our students.
What did we learn as a result of the discussion and/or analysis?	Students are progressing in identifying details. The reading strategies we have been using seem to be working. Initially students struggled with even locating details (initial assessment data). These midpoint assessment results show that they can find details, but need support in figuring out what is important and then how to use that information to determine the main idea.
How did this change the way we currently think, or disrupt assumptions we had?	It altered how we look at mastery of learning standards. We used to discuss evidence of student learning, but we would only look at students' ability to master the standard as a whole. Now that we have analyzed the standards, we are able to better diagnose where the learning gaps are.

(Continued)

(Continued)

THIRD-GRADE REFLECTION EXAMPLE

QUESTION	OUR COLLECTIVE REFLECTIONS
How can our learning positively impact my students? How did this help me determine the impact of my instructional decisions?	It is apparent in looking at the data that the time we spent as a team helped us figure out that we had effectively taught our students to identify what key details and main ideas are, but we had not taught them how to figure out whether a detail or idea is important or not. We have been methodical instructionally and have been trying to apply the gradual release of responsibility instructional framework. We will be adding nonexamples to our modeling so that students can see the difference between important and unimportant details and ideas.
What might we need to learn more about? What action(s) will I take as a result of this discussion and/or analysis?	As a team we decided we need to learn more about strategies that help students go deeper with their learning to make decisions about the main idea. Students look to us for confirmation that their details are important and that they have the main idea correct. They don't seem to trust their own judgment. That means we have to give them lots of opportunities to do just that. We are planning on reaching out to our building instructional coach to practice modeling examples and nonexamples of key details and the identification of the main idea. We are going to watch one teacher teach the lesson so that we can talk about the impact on students' learning.

NOTES

_____

_____

_____

_____

TEAM TIME DISCUSSION

Use this template to foster reflective discussion at the close of meetings and other collaborative events (e.g., learning walks).

QUESTION	OUR COLLECTIVE REFLECTIONS
What was our focus of the meeting? Did we keep our dialogue and discussion primarily concentrated on the main focus of the meeting?	
What evidence did we examine?	
What did the evidence tell us about student learning and our teaching?	
What did we learn as a result of the discussion and/or analysis?	
How did this change the way we currently think, or disrupt assumptions we had?	
How can our learning positively impact my students? How did this help me determine the impact of my instructional decisions?	
What might we need to learn more about? What action(s) will I take as a result of this discussion and/or analysis?	

NOTES

Module 16

WHAT DID WE LEARN TODAY?
Build Expert Noticing

PUT THE PLAYBOOK TO WORK FOR YOU

The purpose of this module is to sharpen your expert noticing skills in your own classroom. It also will assist in supporting the thinking of your team members during learning walks (Module 12) and microteaching (Module 13). This module can be used in conjunction with short videos prepared by your professional learning community or with commercially prepared videos of teaching and learning. Developing expert noticing skills allows teachers to make informed decisions about their collective next steps in instruction based on students' thinking and understanding. In other words, expert noticing allows teachers to use information about students' learning formatively.

EXPERT NOTICING: HOW IS OUR PLC+ USING STUDENT EVIDENCE OF LEARNING?

One of the characteristics that separate expert teachers from experienced teachers (there is a difference) is the ability to identify the salient evidence in student responses and detach it from extraneous information that does not contribute to a hypothesis of student learning. For instance, novice noticers attend to general instructional strategies, classroom organization, and student behavior, but fail to recall the substantive content of student learning (van Es & Sherin, 2002). Expert noticers, on the other hand, are able to drown out the "noise" of what is happening in a busy classroom to focus on a student's thinking. These expert noticers are able to sort out what's interesting, but not important, from what is dynamic. They are able to see how students are arriving at their understandings, and they ask questions that elicit responses beyond simply being correct or incorrect. More information about expert noticing is in the companion book *PLC+: Better Decisions and Greater Impact by Design.*

◄ **VIDEO 17: MODULE 16 INTRODUCTION**
resources.corwin.com/plcplaybook

EXPERT NOTICING VIDEO PROTOCOL

Select a short video for use with your team. Be sure that the video chosen has substantial student dialogue that can be easily heard. Videos that are closed-captioned are especially useful.

Step 1: Watch the video in full and without interruption. Then replay it and take notes on the following questions. Discuss these briefly as a team to arrive at consensus.

QUESTION	MY THOUGHTS	OUR COLLECTIVE THOUGHTS
What was the teacher trying to accomplish?		
How would you describe the role(s) of the teacher?		
How would you describe the role(s) of the students?		

Step 2: Student Strengths: Now watch the video a third time, and home in on the thinking of the student(s). Do not become distracted by extraneous information, such as the room décor, miscellaneous student behaviors, and general instructional strategies. First focus on the strengths of the students' thinking, using language frames like those below (Jilk, 2016):

"_____ seemed to <u>summarize learning</u> when she or he said _____."

"_____ seemed to <u>organize her or his thinking</u> when she or he said _____."

"_____ seemed to <u>notice a pattern</u> when she or he said _____."

"_____ seemed to <u>transfer learning</u> when she or he said _____."

"_____ seemed to <u>make a hypothesis</u> when she or he said _____."

"_____ <u>pressed for clarification</u> when she or he said _____."

Use the noticing note-taking guide on page 113 to record your thoughts and those of your team.

Step 3: Struggles With Learning: Watch the video a fourth time, this time focusing on evidence of student learning faltering. Language frames can support your noticing:

"_____ expressed confusion when she or he said _____."

"_____ made a factual error when she or he said _____."

"_____ made a procedural error when she or he said _____."

"_____ made a conceptual error when she or he said _____."

"_____ did not notice the error when she or he said _____."

Use the note-taking guide on page 113 to record your thoughts and those of your team.

Step 4: Interpreting Student Thinking: Expert noticers are able to rapidly hypothesize what a student might know and not know that led the student to make a logical error that led to an incorrect response. Chappuis (2014) categorizes errors into three possible types:

- Errors due to incomplete understanding
- Errors due to flaws in reasoning
- Errors due to misconceptions

Given your observation of errors, what type(s) of errors are you primarily seeing in the video? Use the note-taking guide on page 113 to record your thoughts and those of your team.

Step 5: Recommendations for Responses: When confronted with a similar situation, what recommendation would you make for responding? What scaffolds might be useful in this circumstance to assist the learner in arriving at a correct answer or drawing an accurate conclusion? Possible scaffolds include the following (Frey & Fisher, 2010):

- Background knowledge prompts (e.g., "Think about what you already know about mammals.")
- Process or procedural prompts (e.g., "Go back and look at your first step. Did you follow the correct order of operations?")
- Prompts to try another strategy (e.g., "Try rereading that last paragraph, and this time make a list of the reasons the author gives.")
- Asking reflective questions (e.g., "How would you expect one of the protesters in this march to react to the military's use of force?")

The failure of students to uptake a prompt may indicate that reteaching is necessary. However, the response should be an attempt to get the student(s) to engage in the cognitive and metacognitive thinking required. It should be noted that providing scaffolding is an issue of expectations and equity as well, especially as it intersects with gender (Sadker, 2002), race (McAfee, 2014), and immigration status (Planas & Gorgorió, 2004).

TEAM TIME DISCUSSION

Expert noticing develops with practice and is best applied in your own classroom. How might you foster your own continued professional learning on expert noticing? What steps might your team take to learn together? Use the discussion questions below to consider steps you and your team will take.

QUESTION	MY THOUGHTS	OUR COLLECTIVE THOUGHTS	COMMITTED ACTIONS
How can the development of expert noticing impact our classroom practice(s)?			
What will I be mindful of as I interact with students?			
How might I use the collective knowledge of my team to improve my expert noticing?			
What human and material resources can we access to further develop our expert noticing skills?			

NOTICING NOTE-TAKING GUIDE

	MY THOUGHTS	OUR COLLECTIVE THOUGHTS
Step 1: Initial viewing of video		
Step 2: Evidence of student learning strengths		
Step 3: Evidence of student errors or misconceptions		
Step 4: Interpretation of student thinking		
Step 5: Recommendations for responses		

NOTES

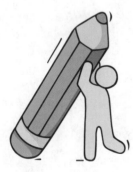

Module 17

WHAT DID WE LEARN TODAY?
Common Assessments

PUT THE PLAYBOOK TO WORK FOR YOU

The focus of this module is on developing a common assessment for the team to use to gauge the impact of your teaching, and to design future instruction. Common assessments are tests or assessment items administered to all students of teachers within a PLC+. The purpose is for team members to all have a similar measure of student learning for comparison. They are useful for calibration purposes as well, as you need agreement about the standards or learning objectives you will assess in addition to how you will assess them. Evidence of learning allows the team to develop targeted instructional adjustments. Common assessments are administered at the beginning and at the end of a unit of study, and are aligned to the common challenge identified by the team in Module 8 on page 69.

COMMON ASSESSMENTS/ QUALITY ASSESSMENT EVIDENCE

There is no single assessment or item type that will provide all the information needed to gauge student learning. Therefore, common assessments typically involve a mixture of assessment item types. Each has advantages and disadvantages. Teams can increase the value of their reflections about their own learning by considering the quality of evidence they gather through the common assessments they design.

◀ **VIDEO 18: MODULE 17 INTRODUCTION**
resources.corwin.com/plcplaybook

ASSESSMENT ITEM TYPE	ADVANTAGES	DISADVANTAGES
Multiple-choice questions	Quick and easy to score, by hand or electronically Can be written so that they test a wide range of higher-order thinking skills Can cover lots of content areas on a single assessment yet still be answered in a class period	Often test literacy skills, even when those are not the focus of the assessment Provide unprepared students the opportunity to guess; correct guesses can be misinterpreted as evidence of student knowledge Expose students to misinformation that can influence subsequent thinking about the content Takes time and skill to construct valid questions and distractors
True-false questions	Quick and easy to score Allow for surface-level comparison between concepts	Considered to be one of the most unreliable forms of assessment due to false dichotomies Often written so that most of the statement is true save one small, often trivial bit of information that then makes the whole statement untrue Encourage guessing; correct guesses can be misinterpreted as evidence of student knowledge
Short constructed response questions	Quick and easy to write Quick and easy to grade Offer some insights into students' thinking and rationale	Can encourage students to memorize terms and details at the expense of deep learning, such that their understanding of the content remains superficial

ASSESSMENT ITEM TYPE	ADVANTAGES	DISADVANTAGES
Essay questions	Offer students an opportunity to demonstrate knowledge, skills, and abilities in a variety of ways Can be used to develop student writing skills, particularly the ability to formulate arguments supported with reasoning and evidence	Require extensive time to grade Somewhat subjective criteria used when assessing answers (e.g., content versus mechanics and conventions) If used as timed writing, necessitate quick composition with less time for planning or revision If used as an out-of-class assignment, can expose inequities of access to environmental and technological resources If used as an out-of-class assignment, answers may reflect outside assistance or plagiarized content rather than the student's knowledge
Questions provided by test banks	Save teacher time and energy involved in writing test questions Use the terms and methods that are used in the textbook or commercial curricula Provide students some (forced) choice when determining correct or best answers on assessment	Rarely involve analysis, synthesis, application, or evaluation—most questions are recall and reproduction items Limit the scope of the assessment to text content; if used extensively, may lead students to conclude that cross-disciplinary applications are unimportant

Source: Adapted from "This Is Only a Test: A Machine-Graded Improvement to the Multiple-Choice and True-False Examination" by D. McAllister and R. M. Guidice (2012), in *Teaching in Higher Education, 17*(2), 193–207. Used with permission.

DESIGN A COMMON ASSESSMENT TO USE FOR PREUNIT AND POSTUNIT COMPARISONS

Common assessments are used at the beginning and end of a unit of study to create a means for measurement of progress and achievement. Common assessments can be developed as a whole, or embedded in a summative assessment instrument. In addition, the common assessment should be designed such that it helps your team answer the common challenge your team identified in Module 8.

A note about students. Students may not be familiar with the nature and purpose of common assessments, so be sure to explain that the results are used by you and your team to improve your practice and their learning. Assure them that the results of the initial assessment are not a part of their grade for the class, and are used exclusively by your team for your professional learning.

NOTES

_____

_____

_____

_____

_____

_____

_____

_____

_____

_____

_____

_____

_____

_____

_____

_____

_____

_____

_____

TEAM TIME DISCUSSION

Common Challenge	
What assessment format(s) will we use?	
Items for preunit/postunit assessments	
Date of administration of preunit common assessment	
Date of team discussion of preunit assessment results (use data analysis protocol in Module 8)	
Date of postunit administration of common assessment	
Date of team discussion of postunit assessment results (use data visualization tool in Module 18)	

NOTES

Module 18

WHAT DID WE LEARN TODAY?

Determining Impact and
Comparing Progress
and Achievement

PUT THE PLAYBOOK TO WORK FOR YOU

The purpose of this module is to determine impact and visualize student progress and achievement data. To do so, you will need initial or preunit assessment data as well as postunit assessment data. You will also need to download a tool to use that will create visual representations of the data, allowing your team to determine student needs. A QR code to do this is provided on page 122 under "Visualizing Data."

DETERMINING IMPACT

Teaching should impact learning. And teams need to determine the impact that they have on individual students as well as groups of students. An effect size calculator is an easy way to determine the impact that you have on students' learning. Effect size measures order of magnitude; in this way it is comparable to the Richter scale for earthquakes. Some effects are barely noticed (e.g., effects with an effect size of 0.10 or less), and others are strong (e.g., effects with an effect size of 0.80 or greater). The tool you will use in this module calculates effect sizes for each individual student and for the group. Teams can use this information to determine why some students are not making progress and act quickly.

PROGRESS VERSUS ACHIEVEMENT

You recognize that achievement is important. You want all students to achieve mastery of the grade-level or content standards. Accountability assessments are created to determine which students have achieved the expected level of performance and which have not. But we also believe that progress is important. A student who is performing well below the expectation but who makes

◀ **VIDEO 19: MODULE 18 INTRODUCTION**
resources.corwin.com/plcplaybook

significant progress is different from a student who is not performing well and who does not make progress. Progress and achievement do not have to be at odds with one another. Instead, there are four quadrants that allow educators to consider actions based on both progress and achievement.

HIGHER ACHIEVEMENT, LIMITED PROGRESS	**HIGHER ACHIEVEMENT, SIGNIFICANT PROGRESS**
LOWER ACHIEVEMENT, LIMITED PROGRESS	**LOWER ACHIEVEMENT, SIGNIFICANT PROGRESS**

VISUALIZING DATA

◄ **VISUALIZING DATA**
resources.corwin.com/plcplaybook

This QR code will allow you to download an Excel file that you can use to create the visuals.

Notice that there are tabs for 30, 50, and 100 students. Enter each student's data, both preunit and postunit assessment information. The system will calculate the effect size for each student and the whole group. The system will also calculate the average achievement for the cohort and then plot students in the appropriate quadrant. When using effect sizes to discuss student progress and achievement, it is important to move beyond just looking at the numbers (effect sizes) and focus more on what has impacted the numbers.

In the remaining modules in this Playbook, the data will be analyzed for gaps between groups of students, and equity implications will be explored. For now, team discussions should focus on what was learned from the data about your teaching and the needs of students moving forward.

Teams have two options for discussion of these data. The first focuses on the effect sizes, and the second focuses on progress and achievement. Some teams create a hybrid of these sources to talk about trends and barriers to learning for individual students.

TEAM TIME DISCUSSION

Using the effect size information, consider the following questions.

Common Challenge

QUESTION	MY THOUGHTS	OUR COLLECTIVE THOUGHTS
What is the overall impact of the unit? Is it sufficient, or do we need to make changes?		
What changes did we implement during the course of the unit? What impact did those changes have?		
Which students had negative growth? Why do we think that is? What do we need to do about it?		
Which students had minimal growth? Why do we think that is? What do we need to do about it?		
Which students had exceptional growth? Why do we think that is? What do we need to do about it?		

TEAM TIME DISCUSSION

Using the progress and achievement visuals, consider the following questions.

Common Challenge

QUESTION	MY THOUGHTS	OUR COLLECTIVE THOUGHTS
In which quadrant are the majority of students? Why do we think that is?		
Why did some students not make the expected progress?		
What barriers exist for students?		
What have we tried during the unit that did, or did not, work?		
What did we learn about the instructional experiences we provided for students from analyzing the data this way?		
What implications do the data have for our common challenge?		

Module 19

WHAT DID WE LEARN TODAY?
Crosscutting Values Check

PUT THE PLAYBOOK TO WORK FOR YOU

The purpose of this module is to revisit the crosscutting values of the PLC+ framework and determine the ways in which they are realized in your work. The crosscutting values check allows teams to make adjustments to improve learning for students and teachers. We begin with a discussion about the roadblocks some teams have to talking about learning.

EQUITY AND EXPECTATIONS VALUES

The core values of the PLC+ framework include equity and expectations. Without these values, student learning varies considerably, and often students are blamed for their lack of progress or achievement. Members of a PLC+ team assume responsibility for the learning of all students and are willing to talk honestly, and openly, about how they can best meet the needs of all of their students. When we directly discuss the values of equity and expectations, we may uncover assumptions that need to be addressed. The checklist on page 128 provides some questions that PLC+ teams have found useful in checking in on their values.

OVERCOMING OBSTACLES TO TALKING ABOUT LEARNING

As teams discuss the fourth guiding question, "What did we learn today?" conversations focus on teaching practices, pedagogy, and student learning at deep levels. Sometimes, teams are reluctant to discuss learning and the roadblocks that exist to students' learning. "Rich and recurring discourse promotes high standards of practice, and both generate and reinforce core beliefs,

◀ VIDEO 20: MODULE 19 INTRODUCTION
resources.corwin.com/plcplaybook

norms, and values of the community. In other words, talk is the bridge between educational values and improved practice in schools" (Horn & Little, 2009, p. 82). The following are potential roadblocks that teams face as they attempt to discuss learning. As a PLC+ team, how might you develop some actions to avoid these pitfalls?

ROADBLOCKS TO TALKING ABOUT LEARNING	DESCRIPTION	HOW CAN YOUR PLC+ AVOID THIS ROADBLOCK?
Fear of Incompetence	PLC+ members have an innate desire to not look foolish or less than 100 percent competent in all aspects of teaching responsibilities. Thus, they are at times reluctant to share ideas, inferences, or suggestions.	
Peacocking	PLC+ members restate similar ideas of other individuals to validate their stance, or to simply add their voice to the conversation.	
Pecking Order	There is a real or perceived belief that certain members of the PLC+ team hold more power, authority, or expertise than others, and thus their voices carry much more weight and stifle the team's overall ability to learn and become collectively efficacious.	

ROADBLOCKS TO TALKING ABOUT LEARNING	DESCRIPTION	HOW CAN YOUR PLC+ AVOID THIS ROADBLOCK?
Rationalizing Ineffective Practice	Certain practices are deemed (inaccurately) to be effective, and this is done without the team examining evidence or a rationale for implementing these practices. Often team members avoid challenging certain notions based on the individuals who are suggesting them.	
Alliances	Team members form alliances with peers of like thought or who prefer similar approaches. They voice agreements or disagreements based on these alliances and not on evidence of effectiveness of teaching practices.	
Learned Helplessness	Team members normalize challenges and obstacles to unhealthy and detrimental levels. They acknowledge challenges in student learning as being common, but rationalize them as a product of unconquerable circumstances, rather than opportunities that challenge the team and that can collectively be tackled over time.	

EQUITY AND EXPECTATIONS VALUES CHECKLIST

QUESTION	MY THOUGHTS	OUR COLLECTIVE THOUGHTS
Did we take time to reflect on students' learning?		
Did we take time to reflect on our own learning?		
What evidence do we have about students' learning?		
Have we developed and administered common assessments that will allow us to determine mastery and needs for additional learning?		
What did we learn about our impact on students?		
What did the progress versus achievement exercise teach us?		
What do we need to modify in our plan that will allow us to address the common challenge?		

ACTIVATE LEARNING FOR MYSELF AND OTHERS CHECKLIST

Student learning needs drive adult learning needs. Once teams understand where students are now in their learning journey, teams need to take a step back to reflect on their personal learning. Are there any adult learning needs that must be met to best be able to support student learning? As already discussed, the + in the PLC+ is you, and so it is important to recognize learning for teachers is a constant. Given that you want to move student learning forward, what learning do you (or your team) need to accomplish to ensure that all students are successful?

WHAT DID WE NOTICE AS OUR STUDENTS ENGAGED IN THIS LEARNING UNIT?	WHAT ARE MY LEARNING NEEDS SO I CAN MEET MY STUDENTS' LEARNING NEEDS? What strategies might I need to learn more about?	WHAT LEARNING WILL I ENGAGE IN TO MEET MY LEARNING NEEDS? What will I do on my own? What can I do with colleagues?

COLLECTIVE EFFICACY CHECKLIST

Teams that are empowered to make decisions, act, communicate clearly, and hold themselves accountable for their efforts manifest high degrees of collective teacher efficacy (CTE). Use the checklist below to gauge and monitor the actions that will follow your work about the fourth question, "What did we learn today?"

QUESTION	MY THOUGHTS	OUR COLLECTIVE THOUGHTS
How confident are we in the assessments we used to determine students' progress?		
Do we believe that our team and our school are moving in a positive direction to improve student learning?		
How has our team's learning transferred to teacher practice?		
What experiences do we need to have to extend our sense of collective efficacy?		

Module 20

GUIDING QUESTION 5: WHO BENEFITED AND WHO DID NOT BENEFIT?

PUT THE PLAYBOOK TO WORK FOR YOU

This final section focuses on the fifth guiding question in the PLC+ framework, "Who benefited and who did not benefit?" This is an opportunity for your team to look for hidden inequities (and those hiding in plain sight) as you revisit the progress and achievement data compiled in Module 18 on page 122. This examination begins with locating patterns of unequal progress within your own classroom. It creates a platform to explore your own teaching effectiveness as you identify those students with whom you have had success, and those you have not yet reached. The module then shifts to team analysis of results.

PLC+ Framework Guiding Questions

1. **Where are we going?**

2. **Where are we now?**

3. **How do we move learning forward?**

4. **What did we learn today?**

5. **Who benefited and who did not benefit?**

◄ **VIDEO 21: MODULE 20 INTRODUCTION**
resources.corwin.com/plcplaybook

ON YOUR OWN

Use the data visualization completed in Module 18, and focus now on the results for the students you taught. Complete the grid on page 135 and use the reflective questions that follow to prompt your reflective thinking. We have completed a sample for you as a model of how you might display the data on a spreadsheet.

Mr. Lorenzo Period 1—Biology

Unit 2 Preunit and Postunit Assessment Comparison

ASSESSMENTS WERE A MIXTURE OF MULTIPLE-CHOICE, CONSTRUCTED RESPONSE, AND EXTENDED RESPONSE QUESTIONS					
STUDENT	PREUNIT ASSESSMENT PERFORMANCE LEVEL AND SCORE	POSTUNIT ASSESSMENT PERFORMANCE LEVEL AND SCORE	MASTERY (YES/NO)	GROWTH (YES/NO)	CURRENT GRADE IN COURSE
Katie A.	Beginning 3/36	Proficient 21/36	No	Yes	C
Latrice C.	Proficient 28/36	Proficient 23/36	No	No	A
Marcus E.	Approaching 19/36	Proficient 22/36	No	Yes	B
Amelia F.	Approaching 15/36	Beginning 9/36	No	No	F
Michael F.	Proficient 21/36	Mastery 30/36	Yes	Yes	B
Eduardo H.	Beginning 3/36	Proficient 21/36	No	Yes	C

STUDENT	PREUNIT ASSESSMENT PERFORMANCE LEVEL AND SCORE	POSTUNIT ASSESSMENT PERFORMANCE LEVEL AND SCORE	MASTERY (YES/NO)	GROWTH (YES/NO)	CURRENT GRADE IN COURSE
Loren J.	Proficient 24/36	Proficient 29/36	No	Yes	A
Vanessa L.	Approaching 16/36	Approaching 19/36	No	Yes	B
Lawrence L.	Proficient 27/36	Proficient 23/36	No	No	A
Jose M.	Proficient 28/36	Mastery 30/36	Yes	Yes	B
Michael M.	Mastery 32/36	Mastery 32/36	Yes	No	A
Sarah P.	Proficient 29/36	Proficient 27/36	No	No	B
Natasha P.	Beginning 8/36	Approaching 16/36	No	Yes	D
Nate R.	Approaching 12/36	Approaching 19/36	No	Yes	C
Clarence R.	Proficient 21/36	Approaching 19/36	No	No	B
Li R.	Proficient 21/36	Proficient 26/36	No	Yes	A

(Continued)

(Continued)

STUDENT	PREUNIT ASSESSMENT PERFORMANCE LEVEL AND SCORE	POSTUNIT ASSESSMENT PERFORMANCE LEVEL AND SCORE	MASTERY (YES/NO)	GROWTH (YES/NO)	CURRENT GRADE IN COURSE
Thomas S.	Approaching 19/36	Proficient 24/36	No	Yes	B
Miosha T.	Beginning 15/36	Proficient 22/36	No	Yes	C
Dwayne V.	Mastery 31/36	Mastery 30/36	Yes	No	A

OVERALL GROWTH SUMMARY FROM PREUNIT TO POSTUNIT ASSESSMENT

Beginning: 4/4 students grew either one or two performance levels from pre to post

Approaching: 3/5 students regressed a level; 1/5 students stayed the same; 1/5 students grew one performance level

Proficient: 1/8 students regressed a level; 5/8 students stayed the same; 2/8 students grew one performance level

Mastery: 2/2 students stayed at this level

PREUNIT ASSESSMENT	POSTUNIT ASSESSMENT
Beginning: 4/19 students	Beginning: 2/19 students
Approaching: 5/19 students	Approaching: 4/19 students
Proficient: 8/19 students	Proficient: 9/19 students
Mastery: 2/19 students	Mastery: 4/19 students

DATA REVIEW

CLASS:

UNIT:

ASSESSMENT:

STUDENT	PREUNIT ASSESSMENT PERFORMANCE LEVEL AND SCORE	POSTUNIT ASSESSMENT PERFORMANCE LEVEL AND SCORE	MASTERY (YES/NO)	GROWTH (YES/NO)	CURRENT GRADE IN COURSE

ON YOUR OWN

REFLECTIVE QUESTION	YOUR RESPONSES
What type of growth and achievement did you see from all of your students? Why might that be?	
Did some students grow but not achieve an expected level of mastery? Are there patterns you can detect?	
Did some students achieve mastery on the postunit assessment but not grow from their preunit assessment score to the one they received on the postunit assessment? Are there patterns you can detect?	
Using the effect size data generated, who were you most effective with? Who were you least effective with?	
What initial conclusions have you drawn from your analysis of the data?	
What questions do you want to pose to your team?	

EQUITY AUDIT PROTOCOL: REVISIT THE DATA AS A TEAM

Using the individual results you and your team members prepared, discuss the results you have found and the questions you would like to pose to your colleagues. Because there are often patterns in findings, it is wise to begin with a roundtable of results and questions. The appointed activator for this data analysis is charged with keeping the process moving forward. If there is a team member who does not have direct classroom responsibilities, he or she can serve as the activator.

Step 1: Roundtable: Each team member briefly shares the results of his or her analysis with the group. Use the notes you prepared to support your presentation of the data. (3 minutes for each participant)

- Number of students who made progress and demonstrated mastery
- Number of students who made progress but did not demonstrate mastery
- Number of students who did not make progress and demonstrated mastery
- Number of students who did not make progress and did not demonstrate mastery
- One or two patterns you discovered in your analysis
- One question you have for the team

NOTES

_____

_____

_____

_____

_____

_____

_____

_____

_____

_____

_____

_____

_____

Step 2: Identification of Common Results and Questions: After listening to each brief classroom data overview in the roundtable, identify common themes related to results, as well as questions that resonate with the group. (5 minutes)

COMMON THEMES

1.

2.

3.

QUESTIONS RAISED BY THE DATA

1.

2.

3.

Step 3: Dig Deeper to Uncover Patterns of Inequality: Use the questions listed below to reexamine your data in light of possible patterns. While some of the more common patterns are often identified early on (e.g., patterns among the scores of English learners), others may appear later and shed new light on your results (e.g., patterns that are related to attendance). (30 minutes)

CHARACTERISTIC	EQUITY GUIDING QUESTION	EMERGING PATTERNS
Attendance	Do the learners within each quadrant have similar attendance habits? Challenges with truancy or tardiness?	
Interest	How do the learners' explicit or implicit interests in reading correspond to the quadrants?	
Transience and Mobility	Are learners that joined the class late or later in the year experiencing the same achievement and growth as those students that have been members of the class/school the entire year or years?	
Gender	What is the distribution of males and females across the quadrants?	
Socioeconomic Status	Are children in poverty showing differential levels of achievement and or growth?	
Race	What is the distribution of races across the quadrants?	
Ethnicity	How does the ethnic makeup of the grade level show up in each quadrant?	
Disability Status (IEP and 504)	Do students with an identified disability progress and achieve in this classroom and grade level?	
English Language Learners	Are children learning English as a subsequent language showing differential levels of achievement and/or growth?	

Step 4: Examine Issues of Access: Some students fail to make progress, or fail to master content, due to issues of access. These are not always apparent, but they can be pervasive. There is a saying that "the last thing a fish notices is the water it swims in," and so it can be with barriers to access. Take time to interrogate these less obvious access issues that can interfere with and inhibit student growth and learning. (20 minutes)

QUESTION	MY THOUGHTS	OUR COLLECTIVE THOUGHTS
Are we really offering each learner equitable access and opportunity for all learning intentions and success criteria?		
Have we maintained high expectations for all students regardless of where learning began?		
Are there organizational or institutional barriers that are hindering the growth of some?		

Step 5: Use Results, Patterns, and Access to Address the Common Challenge: Your team's further analysis of the results of your efforts, especially through an equity lens, will naturally prompt discussion of responses. We ask that you pause before developing future plans, in order to return to your common challenge. (15 minutes)

Common Challenge

QUESTION	MY THOUGHTS	OUR COLLECTIVE THOUGHTS
Who is currently benefiting from our instruction?		
Who is not benefiting from our instruction?		
What do these results suggest as they relate to our common challenge?		
What questions remain related to our common challenge?		

Step 6: How Do We Strengthen Our Practice? Results are feedback to you about the impact of your teaching (Hattie, 2012). Although this can be a sensitive topic, it is vital to address it in your journey as an effective educator. Imagine what would happen if a doctor never bothered to find out whether his or her patients responded favorably to treatment! Discuss how the results are prompting reflection about your individual practice, and that of the PLC+ team as a whole. (20 minutes)

QUESTION	MY THOUGHTS	OUR COLLECTIVE THOUGHTS
What are the implications for our individual practice?		
In what ways might these results inform future inquiry by our team?		
What have we learned that can strengthen our PLC+ moving forward?		

Step 7: What Actions Are We Compelled to Take on Behalf of Students? In light of your investigation of the data, what action steps will your PLC+ team take to improve future student learning? *Any one of these goals holds the potential of being your next common challenge.* (20 minutes)

GOALS	PROPOSED ACTION	INTERNAL SUPPORTS WE WILL NEED	EXTERNAL SUPPORTS WE WILL NEED	DATE TO REVISIT (MONITOR PROGRESS)
To improve equitable access to content				
To improve teacher clarity				
To improve teacher credibility				
To strengthen expectations				
To remove organizational or institutional barriers				

NOTES

Module 21

WHO BENEFITED AND WHO DID NOT BENEFIT?

Responding to Improve Student Learning

PUT THE PLAYBOOK TO WORK FOR YOU

Your analysis of results has shone a spotlight on students who are not progressing and/or who are not reaching mastery. In this module, you will examine your team's plans for supporting students moving forward. The intent of this module is *not* to identify individual students for intervention. Your school or district may have a process already in place for doing so. The purpose of this module is evaluating your current Response to Intervention (RTI) system, or tiered intervention, and reformulating it to reflect your team's learning.

THE VITAL NATURE OF PROGRESS MONITORING

The work your PLC+ team has accomplished in looking carefully at the results data is a form of progress monitoring. You intentionally sought to identify students who are not making progress under current conditions. Of course, it doesn't end there. It is crucial that educators respond to gaps in learning. The protocol featured in this module is designed to assist your team in looking carefully at your current RTI, or tiered intervention, system and to determine areas for improvement:

- Tier 1 quality core instruction
- Tier 2 supplemental interventions
- Tier 3 intensive supports

More information about tiered interventions can be found in the companion book *PLC+: Better Decisions and Greater Impact by Design* on pages 162–169.

◄ **VIDEO 22: MODULE 21 INTRODUCTION**
resources.corwin.com/plcplaybook

TIERED INTERVENTION PROGRESS MONITORING PROTOCOL

TIER 1

Suggested Time: 20 minutes

Purpose: Tier 1 quality core instruction is central to intervention. Without quality core instruction, intervention efforts are quickly overwhelmed by the sheer volume of students in need of better instruction. Therefore, the initial discussion should always center on Tier 1 first.

QUESTION	MY THOUGHTS	OUR COLLECTIVE THOUGHTS
What evidence do we have that all students are receiving high-quality, evidence-based instruction?		
How do we monitor ourselves to ensure delivery of high-quality instruction?		
What is indicated by the assessment results and analysis of student errors? Did interpretation of the results identify gaps?		
If an intervention is currently in place for some students, what can we discern about their learning from the existing data?		

ACTIONS TO STRENGTHEN TIER 1 QUALITY CORE INSTRUCTION

Use the sentence frames below to assist you in developing an action plan.

- If we do _____, then _____ will be the potential impact.
- Data that support our decisions include _____.
- The student benefits of our actions will be _____.

146

Suggested Time: 30 minutes

Purpose: Tier 2 supplemental interventions are supports delivered in the classroom by the teacher and, at times, by external personnel (e.g., bilingual support specialist, instructional coach). Examine the current status of Tier 2 supports in your team, and the extent to which they are being effectively organized, delivered, and monitored.

QUESTION	MY THOUGHTS	OUR COLLECTIVE THOUGHTS
What current Tier 2 supports are in place?		
How are we monitoring the effectiveness of our Tier 2 efforts?		
Do our current Tier 2 efforts include social and emotional learning supports for students?		
What unmet needs have we identified?		
What learning does our PLC+ team need in order to improve our Tier 2 efforts?		

ACTIONS TO STRENGTHEN OUR TIER 2 SUPPLEMENTAL INTERVENTION EFFORTS

Use the sentence frames below to assist you in developing an action plan.

- If we do _____, then _____ will be the potential impact.
- Data that support our decisions include _____.
- The student benefits of our actions will be _____.

Suggested Time: 30 minutes

Purpose: Tier 3 intensive interventions are generally delivered outside of the classroom, often in one-to-one arrangements. Examine the current status of Tier 3 supports in your team and the extent to which they are being effectively organized, delivered, and monitored.

QUESTION	MY THOUGHTS	OUR COLLECTIVE THOUGHTS
What current Tier 3 supports are in place?		
How are we monitoring the effectiveness of our Tier 3 efforts?		
Do our current Tier 3 efforts include social and emotional learning supports for students?		
What unmet needs have we identified?		
What learning does our PLC+ team need in order to improve our Tier 3 efforts?		

ACTIONS TO STRENGTHEN OUR TIER 3 INTENSIVE INTERVENTION EFFORTS

Use the sentence frames below to assist you in developing an action plan.

- If we do _____, then _____ will be the potential impact.
- Data that support our decisions include _____.
- The student benefits of our actions will be _____.

Module 22
WHO BENEFITED AND WHO DID NOT BENEFIT?
Crosscutting Values Check

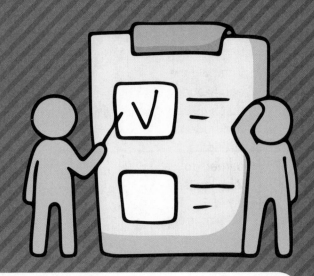

PUT THE PLAYBOOK TO WORK FOR YOU

The purpose of this module is to revisit the crosscutting values of the PLC+ framework and determine the ways in which they are realized in your work. The crosscutting values check allows teams to make adjustments to improve learning for students and teachers.

EQUITY AND EXPECTATIONS VALUES CHECKLIST

The core values of the PLC+ framework include equity and expectations. Without these values, student learning varies considerably, and often students are blamed for their lack of progress or achievement. Members of a PLC+ team assume responsibility for the learning of all students and are willing to talk honestly, and openly, about how they can best meet the needs of all of their students. When we directly discuss the values of equity and expectations, we may uncover assumptions that need to be addressed. The following checklist provides some questions that PLC+ teams have found useful in checking in on their values.

◄ **VIDEO 23: MODULE 22 INTRODUCTION**
resources.corwin.com/plcplaybook

QUESTION	MY THOUGHTS	OUR COLLECTIVE THOUGHTS
What did the equity audit teach us about our students' strengths, barriers to learning, and needs?		
What did the equity audit teach us about ourselves?		
Have we developed plans to remove barriers to students' learning?		
Have we developed intervention plans?		
What have we learned about the PLC+ framework, and what adjustments do we need to make to maximize students' learning?		

ACTIVATE LEARNING FOR MYSELF AND OTHERS CHECKLIST

Student learning needs drive adult learning needs. Once teams understand where students are now in their learning journey, teams need to take a step back to reflect on their personal learning. Are there any adult learning needs that must be met to best be able to support student learning? As already discussed, the + in the PLC+ is you, and so it is important to recognize learning for teachers is a constant. Given that you want to move student learning forward, what learning do you (or your team) need to accomplish to ensure that all students are successful?

WHAT TRENDS DID WE NOTICE ABOUT STUDENTS WHO DID, OR DID NOT, BENEFIT?	WHAT ARE MY LEARNING NEEDS SO I CAN MEET MY STUDENTS' LEARNING NEEDS? What strategies might I need to learn more about?	WHAT LEARNING WILL I ENGAGE IN TO MEET MY LEARNING NEEDS? What will I do on my own? What can I do with colleagues?

COLLECTIVE EFFICACY CHECKLIST

Teams that are empowered to make decisions, take action, communicate clearly, and hold themselves accountable for their efforts manifest high degrees of collective teacher efficacy (CTE). Use the checklist below to gauge and monitor the actions that will follow your work about the fifth guiding question, "Who benefited and who did not benefit?"

QUESTION	MY THOUGHTS	OUR COLLECTIVE THOUGHTS
How confident are we feeling as a team in our instructional abilities?		
How confident are we feeling in removing barriers to student learning?		
How confident are we feeling in our ability to design and deliver effective intervention systems?		
What mastery experiences did we have that built the collective efficacy of our team?		

DEAR EDUCATOR

Congratulations on completing your inaugural cycle of the PLC+ framework! By now we hope you realize that the five questions are not answered in a strictly linear way, but rather provide a structure for moving to action. In fact, you have probably experienced elements of more than one question during a single discussion. We had to present them in some order, which we did. But the order you use to impact students' learning is up to you and your team.

The work of your team continues throughout the year. The common challenge is something that unites or even disrupts current practices. Every good investigation spurs further compelling questions, and we hope that your PLC+ team is feeling renewed, equipped with tools, and confident in your collective ability to address these questions.

We also hope you have gained a new appreciation for the function of a professional learning community. A PLC+ is dynamic and extends far beyond scheduled meetings. It is the embodiment of a vision of an organization working together to increase student learning, build teachers' credibility and clarity, and eliminate inequitable systems and practices.

Finally, our hope is that you have gained a deep understanding of the crucial importance of *you* in the PLC+ system. It is you that makes a difference in the lives of students. But you already knew that. And now you can see that *you* refers both to the individual and to the collective efforts of your team. Football coach Vince Lombardi once observed, "Individual commitment to a group effort——that is what makes a team work, a company work, a society work, a civilization work." Your commitment to yourself and to others is what makes the difference.

Thank you for your service in building the next generation.

—Doug, Nancy, John, Karen, and Dave

REFERENCES

Chappuis, J. (2014). Thoughtful assessment with the learner in mind. *Educational Leadership*, *71*(6), 20–26.

City, E. ., Elmore, R. F., Fiarman, S. E., & Teitel, L. (2009). *Instructional rounds in education: A network approach to improving teaching and learning*. Cambridge, MA: Harvard Education Press.

Donohoo, J. (2017). *Collective efficacy. How educator's beliefs impact student learning*. Thousand Oaks, CA: Corwin.

Frey, N., & Fisher, D. (2010). Identifying instructional moves during guided instruction. *The Reading Teacher*, *64*(2), 84–95.

Goddard, R. D., & Goddard, Y. L. (2001). A multilevel analysis of the relationship between teacher and collective efficacy in urban schools. *Teaching & Teacher Education*, *17*(7), 807–818.

Hattie, J. (2012). *Visible learning for teachers: Maximizing impact on learning*. New York, NY: Routledge.

Hord, S. (2004). Professional learning communities: An overview. In S. Hord (Ed.), *Learning together, leading together: Changing schools through professional learning communities* (pp. 5–14). New York, NY: Teachers College Press.

Hord, S. M. (2007). Learn in community with others. *Journal of Staff Development*, *28*, 39–42.

Horn, I. S., & Little, J. W. (2009). Attending to problems of practice: Routines and resources for professional learning in teachers' workplace interactions. *American Educational Research Journal*, *47*(1), 181–217. doi:10.3102/0002831209345158

Jilk, L. (2016). Supporting teacher noticing of students' mathematical strengths. *Mathematics Teacher Educator*, *4*(2), 188–199.

McAfee, M. (2014). The kinesiology of race. *Harvard Educational Review*, *84*(4), 468–491.

Pasquinelli, E. (2012). Neuromyths: Why do they exist and persist? *Mind, Brain, and Education*, *6*, 89–96.

Planas, N., & Gorgorió, N. (2004). Are different students expected to learn norms differently in the mathematics classroom? *Mathematics Education Research Journal*, *16*, 19–40.

Sadker, D. (2002). An educator's primer on the gender war. *Phi Delta Kappan*, *84*(3), 235–240, 244.

van Es, B., & Sherin, M. G. (2002). Learning to notice: Scaffolding new teachers' interpretations of classroom interactions. *Journal of Technology and Teacher Education*, *10*(4), 571–596.

Wiggins, G. (1998). *Educative assessment*. San Francisco, CA: Jossey-Bass.

A SAGE Publishing Company

Helping educators make the greatest impact

CORWIN HAS ONE MISSION: to enhance education through intentional professional learning.

We build long-term relationships with our authors, educators, clients, and associations who partner with us to develop and continuously improve the best evidence-based practices that establish and support lifelong learning.

3 Ways to get started with PLC+

The **PLC+ framework** is designed to refresh current collaborative structures and support teachers' decision making in the context of individual and collective efficacy, expectations, equity, and the activation of their own learning.

1

Watch the PLC+ Webinar

Preview the PLC+ framework with thought leaders Douglas Fisher and Nancy Frey.

To view the webinar, visit corwin.com/PLCWebinar

2

Attend an Event

Attendees will walk away with a better understanding of the PLC+ framework's potential impact, steps for implementation, and how to build individual and collective efficacy as well as teacher credibility.

For more information, visit corwin.com/PLCInstitutes

3

Meet With a Senior Professional Learning Advisor

Our Senior Professional Learning Advisors will help assess your current PLC structures or discuss options for implementation if your school is new to PLCs. Our customizable PLC+ PD Series ensures better decisions and greater impact by design.

For more information, visit corwin.com/PLCPD

Visit **corwin.com/PLC+** to learn more

CORWIN PLC+